A DISCIPLINARY BLUEPRINT FOR THE ASSESSMENT OF INFORMATION LITERACY

Dorothy Anne Warner

D1318612

LIBRARIES
UNLIMITED
A Member of the Greenwood Publishing Group
Westport, Connecticut • London

Library of Congress Cataloging-in-Publication Data

Warner, Dorothy, 1948–
  An information literacy blueprint for the disciplines / Dorothy Anne Warner.
    p.   cm.
  Includes bibliographical references and index.
    ISBN 978–1–59158–593–0 (alk. paper)
  1. Information literacy—Study and teaching (Higher)   2. Information literacy—Study and teaching
(Higher)—Evaluation.   3. Academic libraries—Relations with faculty and curriculum.
4. Research—Methodology—Study and teaching (Higher)   5. Library orientation for college students.
6. Rider University—Curricula. I. Title.
  ZA3075.W37   2008
    028.7071′1—dc22   2008003775

British Library Cataloguing in Publication Data is available.

Library of Congress Catalog Card Number: 2008003775
ISBN: 978–1–59158–593–0

First published in 2008

Libraries Unlimited, 88 Post Road West, Westport, CT 06881
A Member of the Greenwood Publishing Group, Inc.
www.lu.com

Printed in the United States of America

The paper used in this book complies with the
Permanent Paper Standard issued by the National
Information Standards Organization (Z39.48–1984).

10 9 8 7 6 5 4 3 2 1

To John,
who has inspired many to see what most fail to see

Contents

Preface

This began as a series of brief proposals to my department chairperson, John Buschman, during a developmental leave granted to me by Rider University for the purpose of researching disciplinary information literacy skills and their assessment. I sent the proposals to John throughout my leave to obtain his feedback as to whether they were realistic for our library's instruction program. When he received the third proposal, he commented, "You realize that you're writing a book . . . " to which I replied, "I am?" He recognized the significance of my recommendations for our library's program and suggested that they could be replicated at other institutions. What follows is a more elaborate version of those proposals, but this is still intended to serve as an outline of recommendations for librarians to adapt to their own institutions. I do hope that this framework is one that can be adapted for your institution with the idea that your own creativity and circumstance will determine its success for your students.

The proposals in the chapters ahead are each for a different discipline and provide a framework for both teaching and assessing the students' disciplinary information literacy skills. Each follows a cognitive sequence that has been incorporated within the required courses for the students' disciplinary program. They are, thus, referred to as "sequences," beginning with introductory skills and resulting in the more sophisticated cognitive skills required for the evaluation levels of information literacy.

We've piloted two sequences at Rider University and each has been adapted slightly differently from the original recommendation in response to conversations with faculty in the disciplines. John agreed to "try out" the first sequence with the Sociology Department and Pat Dawson agreed to try out the second sequence with the sciences. Robert Lackie and Diane Campbell are eager to begin the sequences for their disciplines, and I am grateful to all of the instruction librarians for recognizing the good sense of what I am recommending.

Those of us who are lucky enough to work in a library while putting together a manuscript understand the essential role played by the library staff who order books and interlibrary loans, photocopy needed materials, and always understand that the material was needed "yesterday." I appreciate the gracious and good-natured efforts of Carol Beane, Coleen Carr, Mary Ann Dayton, Darlena Dyton, Rose Hilgar, Diane Hunter, and Marianne Lenihan, who were always willing to support yet another request from me. And thank you to Ann Hickey and Doris O'Donovan for their constant support.

Members of the university community have supported my work with assessment for many years. They volunteered their assistance prior to the leave and were willing to be part of the experimental process over the past few months. Thank you to Phyllis Frakt for her leadership of the university's assessment initiatives, for her consistent support of the university libraries, and for her unfailing support of my work; Joe Nadeau for his administrative guidance and support; Barry Truchil and Jim Dickinson for being so willing to incorporate this into their sociology courses; and Reed Schwimmer, Jonathan Karp, and Peter Hester for providing the avenue in the sciences for us to follow. Many faculty members willingly shared their syllabi with me so that I could better develop a sense of their discipline and begin to recognize opportunities for more collaborative approaches to helping the students with their research skills. I cannot speak highly enough of the creativity and collaborative spirit of our faculty at Rider University.

I am deeply grateful to Rider University for granting the developmental leave, which enabled me to develop these proposals, and appreciate the permission granted to me by Rider University to reprint the university materials included here.

Maybe it wasn't the best time to get two very energetic puppies, but Archie and Fergus have given me the excuse to take breaks for many romps around our acre-and-a-half property in New Jersey, which also led, of course, to chats with my neighbors, John Poole and Bob Sutton, who always asked how the manuscript was going. Willie and Angus, two dogs that we've "grown up" with, visited often during this time, and shared the space at my feet with Archie and Fergus while I worked away on the computer. I was always grateful for their company and loyal friendship. And when I was "down to the wire," my son, Josh, willingly took the dogs for many walks so that I could keep going.

And, John, thank you for seeing what I wasn't able to see and for always encouraging me to set the right priorities.

Introduction

In 1994, when I began my job as coordinator of our university's library instruction program, I wanted to know if the students were learning what we were teaching them. It made no sense to me for librarians to expend the energy and time on preparing, teaching, and following up with students if the students were not learning what we expected them to learn.

I developed a research journal for the students to keep, and for me to respond to, and the experience taught me that I had a lot to learn about assessing student learning with a method that would be authentic, yet not cumbersome. This journal idea sat on the back shelf while our instruction program rapidly expanded in response to demand and outreach to professors. These were years of rapid technological change for libraries and a time for librarians to become political players who asserted the need for improved teaching and learning facilities where students could rehearse the skills we were teaching them.

In 2000, I turned my attention once again to assessment of student learning. After all, our accreditors were coming and now we had to prove the learning results of our teaching. A review of assessment literature provided me with definitions of the evaluation and assessment terminology. Mignon Adams (1993, 45) describes "evaluation" as "the systematic gathering of information in order to make decisions." "Formative" evaluation uses techniques such as surveys immediately following instruction, post-tests, or examinations to look at parts or steps of the teaching and learning process with the goal of improving the results of that process. "Summative" evaluation is used to determine the total impact of a program and if an overall program is meeting its goals (Adams, 1993, 47, 49). "Outcomes assessment" looks "not at efforts and expenditures, but their results: to measure changes in performance and behavior. . . . In BI, an outcomes assessment would not be concerned with the number of instructional sessions or the qualifications of the instructor, but rather would consider if students have become better library users as the result of instruction." The focus of the chapters ahead is on "outcomes assessment" and is focused on the bibliographic and information literacy skills of the students in the library instruction program, and thus we refer to "programmatic assessment."

We began our programmatic assessment with the freshman-level students and developed our learning objectives with the freshman-level student in mind (adapted from the Association of College & Research Libraries [ACRL] *Information Literacy Competency Standards for Higher Education* [2000]). These objectives are provided as the first step in the information literacy disciplinary skill development for the teacher preparation majors (Chapter 5). During our pilot with a pre-freshman program (Warner, 2003), we experimented with several assessment tools, including a modified version of the research journal originally developed in 1994. We determined that the journal, which emphasized the process of doing research, served our needs the best and we used the journal as our assessment tool for our formal assessment process.

Adams (1993) identifies several tools or instruments that can be used to answer specific questions related to instruction. She then provides descriptions for the use of the instruments and sources for further information. Although written some years ago, the information she provides continues to be solid.

In addition, I make reference to instruments defined as a "research log" (Chapter 4, Figure 4.2), a "research plan" (Chapter 8, Figure 8.3), and a "research inventory" (Chapter 6, Figure 6.6). These are names used to indicate a "performance measure" that demonstrates what the student has learned during the process of applying bibliographic and information literacy skills. I also refer to a "portfolio" (Chapter 7), which is defined as "a purposeful collection of student work that exhibits the student's efforts, progress, and achievements. The collection must include student participation in selecting contents, the criteria for selection, the criteria for judging merit, and evidence of student self-reflection" (Paulson, cited in Snavely and Wright, 2003, 300).

An example of a rubric is given in Chapter 10. Rubric design was taught to me in a workshop conducted by Donald Ambrose, Rider University, and has become an assessment method that is frequently used in educational environments. The most effective rubrics are designed together by both the teacher and the student so that there is a mutual agreement and understanding of the learning expectations, and how to determine whether one has reached a level of proficiency in an area of learning. The next best situation is to introduce students to the rubric prior to teaching the topic to be learned; this way, again, students can better understand the expectations for learning.

The process of assessing the library instruction portion of the required Research Writing composition courses began in fall 2002. We identified weaknesses in student learning, made teaching improvements, and identified learning improvements with the freshmen over four years (Warner, in press). We adapted an early version of Bloom's Taxonomy of Cognitive Objectives (Bloom et al., 1956) for our assessment rubrics, and determined that the information literacy skill level expectation for freshmen was at the application level of Bloom's Taxonomy. Evaluation of sources and their information content, a skill inherent in all that we teach, is introduced at the freshman level and is considered a progressively learned skill, resulting in students operating at the evaluation level during the junior and senior years of most disciplines.

Thus, we set out to assess the information literacy skills of students in upper-level courses in all the disciplines. I was unable to locate any models for disciplinary teaching and assessment of information literacy skills beyond isolated course examples. While disciplinary standards existed and disciplinary bibliographies existed, there were no developed curricular paths for the teaching and assessment of disciplinary information literacy skills.

Rider University provided a one-semester developmental leave for the research and development of teaching and assessing disciplinary information literacy skills. During that time, I reviewed the curriculum for each discipline at our university, reviewed course syllabi to understand the curriculum sequence for majors in the discipline and the level(s) of information literacy skills currently being taught, conducted a literature review of the information literacy curriculum at other institutions, and a literature review of global trends in the teaching of information literacy. I am not an expert in any of these disciplines, though I have had considerable experience teaching library instruction for English Composition, Communications, and Entrepreneurial Studies. The models that follow are intended to be outlines to be built upon by subject bibliographers. They form the basis for an opportunity for discussion with faculty in the discipline who will offer their own recommendations. The bibliographic outlines and the assignments are from my experience and from the experience of my colleagues and are presented as generically as possible in order to be replicated or to present ideas that can be adapted for your own institution.

Having reached the stage of developing proposals for disciplinary information literacy sequences, I regretted not having done this at the beginning of my library instruction career. Whether you are a seasoned library instruction librarian or one who is just beginning in the field, elements of the models that follow are intended to serve you as a guide. When laying foundational skills for freshmen, we would have benefited from looking at the bigger picture first. We would have been establishing more learning connections for students by identifying how the skills we were teaching to freshmen would directly relate to the skills they would be learning as they progressed in their major.

The writings of early bibliographic instruction librarians continue to inspire me by their richness, depth, and the intellectual grounding of the authors. While in no way an inclusive list, I refer to the work of Beaubien, Hogan, and George; Farber (see Hardesty); Hopkins; Oberman and Strauch; Rawski; Reichel and Ramey; and Wilson. Wherever possible, I have made reference to these sources of inspiration, which have stood the test of time and continue to be relevant for our curricular work today. We need to remember that "bibliography" is at the root of what we do. With this in mind, I have chosen to retain the term "bibliographic" in the descriptions and will at times refer to "bibliographic" and "information literacy" as I believe that we do both. This issue is addressed further in Chapter 2. Some information literacy programs include computer competencies, but the concentration here is on the bibliographic and information literacy sequence.

A definition used for information literacy, as identified in our university's strategic plan, is "an intellectual framework for identifying, finding, understanding, evaluating, and using information. It is integral to all disciplines and to effective teaching, learning, research, and scholarship. The college student should be able to gather, select, and organize quantitative and qualitative information from a variety of sources with an emphasis on those found in a library" (Rider University, 2005). While many interpretations for information literacy exist, the emphasis for our purposes is on an understanding of knowledge production within a discipline, both the content and the context. The process of becoming information literate has its roots in the print bibliographic tradition and an understanding of this tradition underlies the students' abilities to successfully maneuver within the complex, often disorganized, information systems that exist today.

An emphasis on *inquiry* inherent in the active process of information seeking, a process that is frequently not linear and is often interdisciplinary, is at the heart of the student's information literacy skills. The information literacy process will emphasize knowing how to continue the learning process by identifying appropriate information-seeking paths and assessing resulting information sources found.

Inquiry is inherent in the information literacy process. Snavely and Cooper (1997) considered an alternate term, "information inquiry" for information literacy. They noted that, "the two primary meanings of the word *inquiry* are extremely relevant. The first dictionary definition, 'the act or an instance of seeking the truth, information, or knowledge about something: examination into facts and principles: RESEARCH, INVESTIGATION' . . . [Gove, 1986, 1167] names the action of seeking, research, and investigation. It implies evaluation of the information sought and not just an acceptance of any information found (seeking the 'truth'), and it refers to knowledge, which suggests thinking critically about information and incorporating it into what was previously known to create knowledge. The second meaning, 'the act or an instance of asking for information: a request for information: QUERY, QUESTION, [Gove]' focuses on the user and the process of identifying an information need and asking the question. In short, it contains the most important qualities and activities of information-seeking behaviors" (Snavely and Cooper, 1997, 11).

Snavely and Cooper (1997) also considered the term, "literacy." "The context is often what indicates which meaning is appropriate in a particular instance. The definition, 'a person's knowledge of a particular subject or field' [Flexner, 1987, 1122], is clearly more applicable in the context of *information literacy*. An examination of the use of the term *literacy* in the past 30 years clearly indicates that the word is commonly used in this way by many subject areas, that is, a person with a basic interest in and knowledge of the subject or field, but not an expert" (Snavely and Cooper, 1997, 12). Snavely and Cooper note these definitions of "information." "The meanings, 'the communication or reception of knowledge or intelligence' [Gove, 1986, 1160] and 'knowledge communicated by others or obtained from investigation, study, or instruction [Gove] admirably go beyond bits and bytes of data to include the concept of knowledge" (Snavely and Cooper, 1997, 12). The debate about what constitutes information literacy continues and several references for further investigation into the history of bibliographic and information literacy are included in the Additional Readings for this Introduction.

I begin with a "laying the groundwork" section (Chapter 1), which discusses higher education political preparation for librarians. This section also describes the types of resources that were needed in order to begin to develop an understanding of the discipline's curriculum and a path for information literacy within that particular curriculum. What follows (Chapter 2) is a discussion of evaluation and its significance to information literacy and to the upper levels of the curriculum that require a mastery of evaluation skills.

Assessment instruments exist that are well-received by librarians (see Project SAILS/Standardized Assessment of Information Literacy Skills, and see the *iSkills—Information and Communication Technology Literacy Test* developed by the Educational Testing Service). While some "one size fits all" assessment models may be appropriate for introductory-level skills, they do not "fit" for assessing disciplinary information literacy. It is quite different to be information literate in economics than to be information literate in film studies.

For our purposes, assessment is designed to improve teaching in order to improve learning. Each assessment model is specifically designed for programmatic assessment, or assessment in the aggregate. By this, we mean that we are collectively gathering data about student learning of specific information literacy skills, identifying mean scores of the group being assessed, and making teaching improvements in response to the data. This process has proven effective for over four years of programmatic assessment of the information literacy skills of students in the Research Writing classes where we identified improvements in student learning in several areas in response to our teaching improvements (Warner, in press). Several models are provided that are intended to serve as potential frameworks, with the encouragement to adapt these for your particular institution, and with the recognition that all curricular models are intended to be continually in process, and continually reviewed and renewed. Our information literacy instruction program is course-integrated. While the models are for course-integrated instruction, some parallel teaching opportunities have also been suggested. These instruction sessions would link to multiple course assignments. Some models have been linked to the assessment goals of individual disciplines (teacher preparation, communication and journalism, economics, entrepreneurial studies, sociology), one is linked to the program's goals (film studies), one is for a new interdisciplinary science major (The sciences: Integrated sciences and math major), and one is designed for the College of Business Administration and focused on the core requirements for all of its majors.

Curriculum and bibliographic outlines provided with the models are skeletons only and intended to provide a beginning framework. The sources identified are representative and not intended to be an inclusive list. Rubrics are sometimes suggested and a representative rubric is provided (see sociology, Chapter 10). Warner (in press) provides additional illustrations of rubrics used for our freshman-level assessment.

The assessment methods have been developed for a medium-sized institution. Some of the instructional suggestions and their accompanying assessment methods may appear to be difficult to replicate at a larger institution. Larger institutions can consider using random data samples or following a small cohort over an undergraduate experience. Although we are a medium-sized institution, we use sample sizes of data for programmatic assessment and do not attempt to assess each student, though the requirement for the individual student to perform the information literacy skills successfully is real, as it forms part of a course grade. The sample sizes enable us to see our program as a whole for the purposes of improving how and what we teach in order to effect improved learning outcomes by the students.

What I have tried to concentrate on is the fact that research is a process and we must teach to the process and assess the process. The "50-minute BI" cannot occur in isolation. It must clearly be an introduction to the process and the librarians must be available throughout. This may mean cross-training of librarians and a stronger communication built between instruction and reference librarians in order to provide the maximum support for the students. Cross-training in our library is provided by subject specialists for all reference and instruction librarians through workshops, by e-mail, and on the reference desk blog. One workshop taught the market research database, *Choices 3*; detailed instructions are provided by e-mail for our librarians on the use of *Social Sciences Citation Index* so that all librarians are prepared to assist the students. However a library approaches this availability and support for the process will be dependent in part upon the number of librarians available. Creative ways of student support or a restructuring of the library's organization for a student learning focus may be required. We must move away from solely counting the "numbers of sessions that we teach" and consider, too, what the students are learning as a more meaningful interpretation of the value of information literacy within the curriculum. After all, does the number of sessions even mean anything if the students haven't learned what we expected them to? For some of the departments, we recommend individual consultations with students; for a larger institution, the individual consultations could be at the recommendation of the professor in order to have a manageable student group to work with. More than one librarian can be assigned to work with larger numbered groups. Whatever the approach, there must be a commitment to scaffolding, or supporting (Collins, Brown, and Holum, 1991) the student at multiple stages in the development of their learning of bibliographic and information literacy skills. It is not necessary to assess everything all the time, but possible to work with one level or discipline at a time until you are convinced that the students "have it right" and then focus on another group or level, eventually rotating back to the original group.

The development and implementation of disciplinary information literacy sequences will not happen overnight and will require consistent dialog with disciplinary faculty and administrators who share in the assessment process. For some disciplines, assessment of information literacy has been occurring naturally within the discipline, and the important step to be taken is to develop the communication about those results between librarians and faculty in the discipline.

REFERENCES

Adams, Mignon. S. "Evaluation." In *Sourcebook for Bibliographic Instruction*, ed. Katherine Branch, 45–57. Chicago, IL: Association of College and Research Libraries/American Library Association, 1993.

Beaubien, Anne K., Sharon A. Hogan, and Mary W. George. *Learning the Library: Concepts and Methods for Effective Bibliographic Instruction*. New York: R. R. Bowker Company, 1982.

Bloom, Benjamin S., ed., Max D. Engelhart, Edward J. Furst, Walker H. Hill, and David R. Krathwohl. *Taxonomy of Educational Objectives: The Classification of Educational Goals: Handbook I: Cognitive Domain*. New York: McKay, 1956.

Collins, Allan, John Seely Brown, and Ann Holum. "Cognitive Apprenticeship: Making Thinking Visible." *American Educator* 15(3) (Winter 1991): 6–11, 38–46.

Educational Testing Service. *iSkills—Information and Communication Technology Literacy Test*. http://www.ets.org/ictliteracy (accessed March 14, 2008).

Flexner, Stuart Berg. *The Random House Dictionary of the English Language*. 2nd ed. unabridged. New York: Random House, 1987.

Gove, Philip Babcock, ed. *Webster's Third New International Dictionary of the English Language, Unabridged*. Springfield, MA: Merriam-Webster, 1986.

Hardesty, Larry, Jamie Hastreiter, and David Henderson. *Bibliographic Instruction in Practice: A Tribute to the Legacy of Evan Ira Farber*. Ann Arbor, MI: The Pierian Press, 1993.

Hopkins, Frances L. "Bibliographic Instruction as a Liberal Art: An Application of Patrick Wilson's Theory of Pragmatic Bibliography." In *Back to the Books: Bibliographic Instruction and the Theory of Information Sources*, ed. Ross Atkinson, 15–29. Chicago, IL: Association of Research Libraries, American Library Association, 1983.

Oberman, Cerise, and Katina Strauch, eds. *Theories of Bibliographic Education: Designs for Teaching*. New York: R. R. Bowker Company, 1982.

Project SAILS. *SAILS/Standardized Assessment of Information Literacy Skills*. http://www.projectsails.org (accessed September 26, 2007)

Rawski, Conrad H. "On the Nature of Literatures: A Synergetic Attempt." In *Back to the Books: Bibliographic Instruction and the Theory of Information Sources*, ed. Ross Atkinson, 31–56. Chicago, IL: Association of Research Libraries, American Library Association, 1983.

Reichel, Mary, and Mary Ann Ramey, eds. *Conceptual Frameworks for Bibliographic Education: Theory into Practice*. Littleton, CO: Libraries Unlimited, Inc., 1987.

Rider University. *Strategic Plan: 2005–2010*. Lawrenceville, NJ: Rider University, 2005.

Snavely, Loanne L., and Carol A. Wright. "Research Portfolio Use in Undergraduate Honors Education: Assessment Tool and Model for Future Work." *The Journal of Academic Librarianship* 29(5) (September 2003): 298–303.

Snavely, Loanne, and Natasha Cooper. "The Information Literacy Debate." *The Journal of Academic Librarianship* (January 1997): 9–14.

Warner, Dorothy. "Programmatic Assessment of Information Literacy Skills using Rubrics." *Journal on Excellence in College Teaching* (in press).

Wilson, Patrick. "Pragmatic Bibliography." In *Back to the Books: Bibliographic Instruction and the Theory of Information Sources*, ed. Ross Atkinson, 5–14. Chicago, IL: Association of Research Libraries, American Library Association, 1983.

ADDITIONAL READINGS

Arp, Lori. "An Analytical History of 'Library Literacy.'" *RQ* (Winter 1994): 158–163.

Association of College & Research Libraries (ACRL), "Information Literacy Competency Standards for Higher Education." http://www.ala.org/ala/acrl/acrlstandards/informationliteracy competency.cfm (accessed March 13, 2008).

Baker, Betsy, and Mary Ellen Litzinger, ed. *The Evolving Educational Mission of the Library*. Chicago, IL: Bibliographic Instruction Section, Association of College and Research Libraries, A Division of the American Library Association, 1992.

Bawden, David. "Progress in Documentation: Information and Digital Literacies: A Review of the Concepts." *Journal of Documentation* 57(2) (March 2001): 218–259.

Black, Christine, Sarah Crest, and Mary Volland. "Building a Successful Information Literacy Infrastructure on the Foundation of Librarian-Faculty Collaboration." *Research Strategies* 18 (2001): 215–225.

Blixrud, Julia C., and Wanda Dole. "Library Assessment and Performance Measures: An Overview." In *The Bowker Annual: Library and Book Trade Almanac*, ed. Dave Bogart, 273–290. Medford, NJ: Information Today, Inc., 2005.

Bruce, Christine. *The Seven Faces of Information Literacy*. Blackwood, South Australia: Auslib Press Pty. Ltd., 1997.

Bruce, Christine, and Philip Candy, ed. *Information Literacy Around the World: Advances in Programs and Research*. Wagga Wagga, New South Wales: Center for Information Studies, 2000.

Budd, John M. *The Academic Library: Its Context, Its Purpose, and Its Operation*. Englewood, CO: Libraries Unlimited, 1998.

Cameron, Lynn, Steven L. Wise, and Susan M. Lottridge. "The Development and Validation of the Information Literacy Test." *College & Research Libraries* 68(3) (May 2007): 229–236.

Couch, Nena, and Nancy Allen. *The Humanities and the Library*. Chicago, IL: American Library Association, 1993.

Elmborg, James. "Critical Information Literacy: Implications for Instructional Practice." *The Journal of Academic Librarianship* 32(2) (March 2006): 192–199.

Emmons, Mark and Wanda Martin. "Engaging Conversation: Evaluating the Contribution of Library Instruction to the Quality of Student Research." *College & Research Libraries* 63(6) (November 2002): 545–560.

Grassian, Esther S., and Joan R. Kaplowitz. *Information Literacy Instruction: Theory and Practice*. New York: Neal-Schuman Publishers, Inc., 2001.

Hernon, Peter. "Editorial: The Practice of Outcomes Assessment." *The Journal of Academic Librarianship* 28(1) (January–March 2002): 1–2.

Holme, Randal. "Literacy, Historic Development of." In *Encyclopedia of International Media and Communications*, ed. Donald H. Johnston, 61–73. New York: Academic Press, 2003.

Hopkins, Frances L. "A Century of Bibliographic Instruction: The Historical Claim to Professional and Academic Legitimacy." *College & Research Libraries* 43 (May 1982): 192–198.

Iannuzzi, Patricia. "We are Teaching, But Are They Learning: Accountability, Productivity, and Assessment." *Journal of Academic Librarianship* 25 (July 1999): 304.

Jacobson, Trudi E., and Beth L. Mark. "Separating Wheat from Chaff: Helping First-Year Students become Information Savvy." *JGE: The Journal of General Education* 49(4) (2000): 256–278.

Kasowitz-Scheer, Abby, and Michael Pasqualoni. "Information Literacy Instruction in Higher Education: Trends and Issues." *ERIC Digest* ED 465375 (2002). http://www.eric.ed.gov/ERICDocs/data/ericdocs2sql/content_storage_01/0000019b/80/1a/19/45.pdf (accessed July 22, 2006).

Keresztesi, Michael. "The Science of Bibliography: Theoretical Implications for Bibliographic Instruction." In *Theories of Bibliographic Education: Designs for Teaching*, ed. Cerise Oberman and Katina Strauch, 1–26. New York: R. R. Bowker Company, 1982.

Knight, Lorrie A. "The Role of Assessment in Library User Education." *Reference Services Review* 30(1) (2002): 15–24.

Kuhlthau, Carol Collier. *Seeking Meaning: A Process Approach to Library and Information Services*. Norwood, NJ: Ablex Publishing Corp., 1993.

Lindmark, Daniel. "Literacy, Text, Practice, and Culture: Major Trends in the Umea History of Education Research Group, 1972–2002." *Interchange* 34(2/3) (2003): 153–178.

Luke, Allan, "Critical Approaches to Literacy." In *Encyclopedia of Language and Education*, ed. Viv Edwards and David Corson, 143–151. Boston, MA: Kluwer Academic Publishers, 1997.

Maki, Peggy L. "Developing an Assessment Plan to Learn about Student Learning." *The Journal of Academic Librarianship* 28(1) (January–March 2002): 8–13.

Marcum, James W. "Rethinking Information Literacy." *Library Quarterly* 72(1) (January 2002): 126.

Maughan, Patricia Davitt. "Assessing Information Literacy among Undergraduates: A Discussion of the Literature and the University of California-Berkeley Assessment Experience." *College & Research Libraries* 6 (January 2001): 71–72.

McCartin, Marybeth and Paula Feid. "Information Literacy for Undergraduates: Where have we Been and Where are we Going?" *Advances in Librarianship* 25 (2001): 1–27.

McCrank, Lawrence J. "Academic Programs for Information Literacy: Theory and Structure." *RQ* (Summer 1992): 485–497.

Mellon, Constance A., ed. *Bibliographic Instruction: The Second Generation*. Littleton, CO: Libraries Unlimited, 1987.

Mensching, Teresa B. "Trends in Bibliographic Instruction in the 1980s: A Comparison of Data from Two Surveys." *Research Strategies* (Winter 1989): 4–13.

Meulemans, Yvonne Nalani. "Assessment City: The Past, Present, and Future State of Information Literacy Assessment." *College & Undergraduate Libraries* 9(2) (2002): 61–74.

Oberman-Soroka, Cerise. *Petals around a Rose: Abstract Reasoning and Bibliographic Instruction*. Paper presented in the program. "Learning Theory in Action: Applications in Bibliographic Instruction." Chicago, IL: American Library Association, 1980.

Pawley, Christine. "Information Literacy: A Contradictory Coupling." *Library Quarterly* 73(4) (October 2003): 422–452.

Rader, Hannelore B. "From Library Orientation to Information Literacy: 20 Years of Hard Work." In *What is Good Instruction Now? Library Instruction for the 90s*, ed. Linda Shirato, 25–28. Ann Arbor, MI: Pierian Press, 1993.

———. "Information Literacy and the Undergraduate Curriculum." *Library Trends* 44(2) (Fall 1995): 270–278.

———"The Learning Environment—Then, Now and Later: 30 Years of Teaching Information Skills." *Reference Services Review* 27(3) (1999): 219–224.

———. "Information Literacy 1973–2002: A Selected Literature Review." *Library Trends* 51(2) (Fall 2002): 242–259.

Rassool, Naz. "Literacy, Current Status of." In *Encyclopedia of International Media and Communications*, ed. Donald H. Johnston, 49–60. New York: Academic Press, 2003.

Rockman, Ilene F. "Strengthening Connections between Information Literacy, General Education, and Assessment Efforts." *Library Trends* 51(2) (Fall 2002): 185–198.

———. "Editorial: ICT Literacy." *Reference Services Review* 33(2) (2005): 141–143.

Rockman, Ilene F. and Gordon W. Smith. "Information and Communication Technology Literacy." *C&RL News* (September 2005): 587–589.

Ruiter, Jacqueline de. "Aspects of Dealing with Digital Information: 'Mature' Novices on the Internet." *Library Trends* 51(2) (Fall 2002): 199–209.

Savolainen, Reijo. "Everyday Life Information Seeking: Approaching Information Seeking in the Context of Way of Life." *LISR* 17 (1995): 259–294.

Shanbhag, Shilpa. "Alternative Models of Knowledge Production: A Step Forward in Information Literacy as a Liberal Art." *Library Philosophy and Practice* 8(2) (Spring 2006). http://libr.unl.edu:2000/LPP/lppy8n2.htm (accessed June 11, 2006).

Smith, Kenneth R. "New Roles and Responsibilities for the University Library: Advancing Student Learning through Outcomes Assessment." *ARL* 213 (December 2000): 2–5.

Spitzer, Kathleen L. with Michael B. Eisenberg and Carrie A. Lowe. *Information Literacy: Essential Skills for the Information Age*. Syracuse, NY: ERIC Clearinghouse on Information & Technology, 1998.

Street, Brian V. "Social Literacies." In *Encyclopedia of Language and Education*, ed. Viv Edwards and David Corson, 133–141. Boston, MA: Kluwer Academic Publishers, 1997.

Thompson, Gary B. "Information Literacy Accreditation Mandates: What They Mean for Faculty and Librarians." *Library Trends* 51(2) (Fall 2002): 218–241.

Tiefel, Virginia M. "Education for the Academic Library User in the Year 2000." In *Information for a New Age: Redefining the Librarian*, compiled by 15th Anniversary Task Force, Library Instruction Round Table, American Library Association, 57–77. Englewood, CO: Libraries Unlimited, Inc., 1995.

———. "Library User Education: Examining the Past, Projecting its Future." *Library Trends* 44(2) (Fall 1995): 318–338.

Tuominen, Kimmo, Reijo Savolainen, and Sanna Talja. "Information Literacy as a Sociotechnical Practice." *Library Quarterly* 75(3) (2005): 329–345.

Warner, Dorothy Anne. "Programmatic Assessment: Turning Process into Practice by Teaching for Learning." *The Journal of Academic Librarianship* 29(3) (2003): 169–176.

Williams, Janet L. "Creativity in Assessment of Library Instruction." *Reference Services Review* 28(4) (2000): 323–334.

1

Laying the Groundwork

LIBRARIANS AS POLITICAL PLAYERS

In order to be effective, librarians must be political players. Building an information literacy curriculum does not happen overnight. Librarians must first "earn their stripes" by taking academic arguments seriously, developing an understanding of the academic community, becoming involved wherever possible on academic committees, and engaging effectively in shared governance at the university. They must learn to come to the table of each committee meeting with educated opinions.

One must be mindful of the opportunities that exist within one's institution for "making it happen." The deeper the level of institutional involvement and commitment is, the deeper the credibility and, hence, an enabling of academic curricular discussion. There are multiple opportunities for librarians to become involved at many levels in their institution including as active liaisons with their assigned departments. Where librarians hold faculty status, there are opportunities to serve as participants on curricular committees (e.g., general education requirements committees, relevant curricular planning committees, committees dedicated to the freshman experience); as participants in the assessment process (both within the library and within the university); as participants in university planning (e.g., strategic planning task forces); as active participants in the reaccreditation process of the university; as participants in professional development programs within the university; as participants in the university's teaching and learning center; as leaders of organizations within the university, including the American Association of University Professors; and as leaders of both the libraries' and the university's academic policy committees (defined as faculty senates for some institutions).

In many academic institutions, librarians don't have faculty status; some are on contract, some are non-tenure track, some have parallel models, and they may not have access to some committees as a result. This issue was addressed by John Buschman at a LEOX Conference and we note some relevant excerpts from that presentation. "Access alone (e.g., via faculty status) in no way guarantees translating any foothold into effective action for the library in any venue. Conversely, the lack of access does not mean all is lost. . . . Librarians have to have something to contribute to the wider university/college dialog—and not just that which relates to the library or information literacy. Think of it this way: a biologist serving on a curriculum committee is not just there to comment on the role of scientific literacy in the curriculum. S/he is expected to have thought broadly about what an educated person is, what are the necessary (and the desirable) elements of a college education, the balance between general education and learning a field in depth, how much general perspective can be drawn from a major and how much from general education can be applied to the learning in a student's major, and some perspective on students' interests and motivations (or lack thereof). In other words, the biologist is expected to comment as an engaged and informed generalist—not as representing always biology or the sciences generally.

"We bring all of that, too. Think about it. We are as well-equipped to think about curriculum. We have undergraduate and graduate degrees. Via our teaching and public services, we have a unique perspective on the whole curriculum. Our graduate degree in library science has taught us the structure of the literatures of many disciplines. We interact with students at a unique point: the intersection between what they are taught and what they are then expected to apply and teach themselves, and, we hope, their intellectual curiosity.

"Librarians—irrespective of their particular campus status—are involved in the academic enterprise. Learn that, engage it and you will be ready to have an impact on your campus. . . . Too many librarians expect library administrators to take care of all of this. It doesn't work that way—and can't. One or two administrators can't be everywhere, all things to all people, or represent all interests within the library equally well. Additionally, the political realities of top library administrators preclude a large measure of risk-taking or argumentation for a cause. Plus, they do not constitute 'the librarians.' (On the other hand, if you have an administrator who wants to be the only voice, you have a problem that must be tackled before you can be broadly effective as an organization on campus.)

"Though noted earlier, it bears expanding: your participation and interests can not just be from a library perspective. The reason for this will become brutally clear: nobody will care about those issues. You will be balkanized as a special interest, and your broader effectiveness to speak for/on behalf of the library's interests later will be nil.

"I would urge you to think broadly about what you know about your campus' students, curriculum, buildings, revenue sources, climate, benefits, meal plans, HVAC, dormitories, bureaucracy, etc. If the answer is 'not much,' then you cannot realistically expect to have a positive, broad impact for the library. If . . . the answer is 'more than I thought—I just hadn't thought about it that way,' then you have your opening. To place the library as an effective player within a campus means engaging the broader campus context on its own terms (like those just noted) before that context will respond in turn with an understanding and openness to the library's agenda. Being a player in that arena is that important" (Buschman, 2007, reprinted with permission).

A specific example of political involvement related to the sequence for the teacher preparation program follows (in Chapter 5).

BEGINNING THE PROCESS OF INTEGRATING INFORMATION LITERACY INTO THE DISCIPLINES

Developing Curriculum Maps

Several items of documentation were obtained for developing curriculum maps. The current university course catalog identified the course requirements for each major and provided individual course descriptions. A list was created of courses (and professors) that had received library instruction within the past three years. The deans of the colleges provided the names of the professors scheduled to teach in the upcoming academic year (this information could also be provided by the registrars). One college dean also provided data for the total number of sections of the course taught over the past four years. Knowing the scheduled professors and the frequency that the courses are taught assisted in determining the most realistic targets of opportunity.

Using this information, curriculum maps were developed for each major. Elements included in the curriculum maps are not limited, but can include the courses available for the major; whether library instruction has been provided and for whom; the professor(s) scheduled to teach the course; prerequisites for the course; whether any rules apply for the course (e.g., only open to freshmen majoring in business); whether the course is a core course for either the university, college, major or track within the major; the academic level eligible to take the course (freshman, sophomore, junior, or senior); the total number of sections of the course taught; if the syllabi indicated that an information literacy component exists; if the course description in the catalog indicated that an information literacy component exists; if the decision has been made to request course syllabi; who assesses the information literacy component; the type of assessment method used; if the course/professor is to be pursued for information literacy instruction; and (later) the date that the professor was pursued.

These curriculum maps were then adapted for each of the library's disciplinary liaisons into library curriculum maps (Figure 1.1) in order to provide librarians with an overall look at the major and courses (not already receiving library instruction) that represented targets of opportunity. Consideration was also given to the level of involvement that the library currently had with the department/college and whether there existed an opportunity of enriching and deepening the instruction that we already provided. The "opportunity" was determined by whether the course was a requirement for the major, whether it was a core requirement, the professor(s) teaching the course (and how receptive they were to information literacy instruction), the number of sections of the course taught (i.e., the decision was made to target more frequently taught courses first), whether information literacy was identified within the syllabi requirements, or whether the course description in the catalog indicated the possibility for introducing an information literacy requirement.

This provided a wiser approach to developing our information literacy program. Many of our library instruction sessions are taught in elective courses, for professors with whom librarians have good teaching relationships, at the request of the professor, or because librarians have identified an information literacy component in the course and pursued the professor. The goal now is to concentrate on required courses for each major and to develop consistent, sequenced disciplinary instruction that is reinforced at every level. One of our problems over the years has been the unnecessary repetition of instruction for students. While at times this serves the purpose of reinforcing the skills, we recognize that this is not the best use of our energy and that we could provide a much

COURSE (required courses in **bold**)	INFORMATION LITERACY INSTRUCTION PROVIDED (within past 3 years [*] or **Opportunity**)	INFORMATION LITERACY in SYLLABI or CATALOG (* or NA=not applicable)	TOTAL SECTIONS of Course Taught (for past 4 years)	PROFESSORS scheduled to teach course in upcoming academic year
EDU-010-Cohort Seminar (*sophomore level*)	Opportunity	*		*Professor(s) Name*
EDU-100-Contexts of Schooling	*	*	31	*Professor(s) Name*
EDU-200-Developmental Educational Psychology	*	*	31	*Professor(s) Name*
ELD-300-Emergent Literacy P-3	*	*	23	*Professor(s) Name*
ELD-300-Fostering Language & Literacy Development	*	*	22	*Professor(s) Name*
ELD-300-Teaching Math, N-8	*	*	23	*Professor(s) Name*
ELD-300-Teaching Science, Social Studies & Arts	Opportunity	*	22	*Professor(s) Name*
ELD-400-Student Teaching & Seminar	Opportunity	*	6	*Professor(s) Name*
SECONDARY EDUCATION:				*Professor(s) Name*
SED-300-Teaching in the High School (*junior, senior level*)	Opportunity	*	8	*Professor(s) Name*

Unless otherwise noted, course numbers denote the level, 100-level: freshman, 200-level: sophomore, 300-level: junior, 400-level: senior.

Figure 1.1 Curriculum Map for the Teacher Preparation Major.

more productive experience for the students. The curriculum map helped us to develop a path that could provide opportunities for reinforcement of learning while also building the skills of our students. An example of a preliminary curriculum map follows.

From Figure 1.1, it is evident that the professors teaching for the teacher preparation major are receptive to bibliographic and information literacy instruction for their students. The proposal ahead (Chapter 5) identifies two particularly crucial opportunities as anchors for the sequence: the introductory/cohort and senior seminars. What is currently absent from the instruction given to the students in these courses (mentioned in Figure 1.1) is a framework that identifies the curricular continuity of the bibliographic and information literacy instruction. Without this framework, it is difficult to reinforce and to then build upon the skills being learned. It is not enough to have a presence within the discipline. There must be an intentional sequence and purposeful learning links made for the students from one course to the next. Rather than risk duplication of learning and unnecessary repetition from course to course, the intent is to instead *reinforce* the learning. To do this successfully, one must set the context for the new learning situation and bring the earlier concept into that new situation to declare its relevance, thus establishing interrelationships for the learner.

Six proposals have been developed for disciplinary information literacy skill development and their assessment. Where available, the assessment goals and objectives of the department were first identified. In some cases, the disciplinary department may have identified a learning goal that the library can support rather than the library being in the position of recommending the information literacy goal. In some cases, information literacy is included in the existing state or national standards for the discipline (i.e., The Association to Advance Collegiate Schools of Business or AACSB International). Frequently, librarians are required to promote the information literacy needs of disciplinary majors, but just as often, we miss the opportunity to strengthen support for an existing disciplinary goal.

Developing Information Literacy Objectives

Using the departmental assessment goals, disciplinary standards, course descriptions, course syllabi, and disciplinary bibliographic guides, information literacy objectives can be developed for each discipline. Each objective here includes the cognitive level of the skill development according to Bloom's Taxonomy of Cognitive Objectives (a process described in Warner, in press and Warner, 2003, and in Chapter 2, "Evaluation as Inherent in Information Literacy"). With the assessment of the freshman-level information literacy skills, it was determined that freshmen should reach the application level of the taxonomy. Attention was paid in each disciplinary proposal to developing information literacy skills for upper-level students at the analysis, synthesis, and evaluation levels of the taxonomy.

Within each proposal is a further developed curriculum map, which also includes the course description; identification of information literacy course requirements; the information literacy objectives currently addressed in the course; and the cognitive level of information literacy currently expected in the course. A graduated, or progressive, sequence of information literacy skill development, unique to each discipline and building upon required courses for each major, is then proposed. Each proposal includes recommendations for assessing whether the information literacy skill sequence has been successfully learned by the conclusion of the major. Thus, the outline for most proposals includes (a) the assessment goals for the department or program; (b) the professional standards referenced for information literacy (if available); (c) the recommended information literacy objectives to support the discipline (with the cognitive level identified); (d) a best practice (if identified); (e) other relevant reference sources; (f) courses for the major with information literacy requirements (and the cognitive level identified); (g) recommendations for the role of the librarian in sharing the responsibility for teaching the information literacy skills; and (h) recommendations for assessing whether the information literacy skills have been learned.

Librarians are working collaboratively with disciplinary faculty to build upon established teaching relationships, but are now approaching their teaching more deliberately. This is something learned from the assessment process. Rather than operate in a responsive way, which has resulted in a building of support for the information literacy program, librarians are now proactively identifying an information literacy path through each discipline and identifying a cognitive sequence that results in information literacy skill development at the evaluation level of Bloom's Taxonomy in each discipline.

There needs to be a shared responsibility for the teaching and assessing of information literacy skills in order to provide necessary reinforcement. The librarian cannot be the

Information Literacy Skills	Information Literacy Skills	Responsibility
Know	Determines the nature and extent of information needed	Starts with the faculty member; Reinforced by librarians
Access	Efficiently and effectively accesses information sources.	The librarian usually leads, with faculty support.
Evaluate Sources	Critically evaluates information sources.	The librarian may lead initially; Faculty make the ultimate determination from student's work product or performance.
Evaluate Content	Critically evaluates information content; Considers impact on student's prior knowledge, value system, and future direction in life.	Faculty leads in classroom or other course context; Student also may consult librarians, external subject experts, or peers.
Use	Uses information found to accomplish a specific purpose.	Faculty leads; Can be reinforced by librarians.
Ethically/Legally	Understands the economic, legal, and social issues surrounding the acquisition and use of information.	Faculty and librarians jointly and continuously.

Figure 1.2 Shared Responsibilities for Learning.
Source: Middle States Commission on Higher Education 2003, 23. Reprinted with permission.

only one reinforcing the skills. This is where the importance of academic relationships established within the university context comes in. The librarian may have approximately three opportunities for direct contact with the students as a group, while the professor has the opportunity with each contact to reinforce learning. Figure 1.2 (prepared by the Middle States Commission on Higher Education) outlines the shared responsibilities for the teaching and learning of information literacy skills.

Developing the Bibliographic and Information Literacy Curriculum

Once the objectives have been agreed to between the librarians and the disciplinary faculty, the curriculum needs to be developed and integrated with the course material. The proposals ahead are in the process of becoming integrated into the disciplines. We have begun our disciplinary information literacy instruction with the sociology proposal (Chapter 10) and the sciences: integrated sciences and math proposal (Chapter 4) where both librarians and disciplinary faculty reviewed and agreed to the information literacy objectives and were in agreement that the introductory and capstone courses become the focus of the instruction and assessment process. We agreed that there needed to be a connection and reinforcement of skills between these two courses, with additional reinforcement taking place in the intermediate courses.

As with the other proposals, the information literacy curriculum begins with a bibliographic outline. These follow an outline proposed in extensive detail by Beaubien, Hogan, and George (1982), who describe the growth of the discipline and the resulting bibliography for the discipline. They describe the organization of knowledge within a discipline as developing from the stage of pioneering to the stage of elaboration, then proliferation and, finally, the establishment of the discipline. Within each stage, they identify methods of communication, source material, and control tools. Most of the bibliographic outlines that are proposed ahead are organized by primary literature, secondary literature, and tertiary literature. There are different interpretations of secondary literature and tertiary literature. Here we identify secondary literature as including books, text-books, anthologies, peer-reviewed journal articles, professional literature, conference papers, and dissertations. Included in tertiary literature are hybrid tools (encyclopedias and histories), fact tools (statistical sources, handbooks, dictionaries, gazetteers, directories, almanacs, biographical sets, and atlases), guides (to the literature and to reference books), and finding tools (subject guides, bibliographies, catalogs, indexes and abstracts, and Web information seeking). This disciplinary organization of knowledge must be introduced to coordinate with the discipline's curriculum.

In order to identify sources for each category, there are many excellent references that identify the literature for a discipline. The *Reference Sources in the Humanities* series published by Libraries Unlimited was used for the film studies proposal (Chapter 3), and the *Reference Sources in the Social Sciences* series published by Libraries Unlimited was used for the teacher preparation proposal (Chapter 5) and the sociology proposal (Chapter 10). Other disciplinary bibliographies were discovered in searching *Library Literature*, *WorldCat*, and *Amazon.com* using the name of the discipline in combination with "reference sources," "reference literature," "guide," or "information literacy." The references used for each discipline are provided at the conclusion of each disciplinary proposal chapter.

Developing Assessment Methods

While an abundance of assessment methods exist (some of which are identified in the Additional Readings section of the Introduction; see especially Adams, 1993), we have focused on methods that assess the thoroughness of the research process. In the proposals ahead we have attempted to develop methods that coordinated with the curriculum of the discipline and have placed an emphasis on the progressive development of the students' evaluation skills.

Organization of the Proposals

While the proposals are each unique and some more complex than others, each proposal follows a similar outline. Where available, the following information will be provided: assessment goals for the discipline; professional standards referenced for the discipline (noting references to information literacy); best practice identified for information literacy for the discipline; information literacy objectives for the discipline; bibliographic and information literacy curriculum (or sequence or curriculum map) (these are designed by level, i.e., freshman, 100-level, sophomore, 200-level, junior, 300-level, senior, 400-level. In some cases, there will be introductory levels [which may be at the 100- or 200-level], intermediate levels [which may be at either the 200- or 300-level], and advanced level [senior, 400-level]); and assessment methodology. Variations exist in the proposals in order to introduce the opportunity for flexibility within the organizational schema. For example, in one case (Chapter 7), a justification is provided based upon a literature review for the discipline. Assessment methodologies vary depending upon the most logical path for information literacy within the organization of the specific courses required for each major. For some examples, there is assessment at each level; for others (as with sociology, Chapter 10, for example), students are assessed in the introductory (sophomore, 200-level, in this case) and capstone (senior, 400-level) courses. The example for the entrepreneurial program is defined as "natural assessment" as it occurs naturally, i.e., as the students in this program develop their small business plans, the credibility of their proposals rests on the evidence that they have identified (e.g., industry trends, consumer data). The quality of the plan will depend upon the quality of the information located, so the assessment of the student's information literacy skills is "naturally" built in to the overall assessment of the student's business plan. In this case, the library is not responsible for the actual assessment, but is responsible for responding to the feedback from the professors related to student research requirements.

REFERENCES

Adams, Mignon S. "Evaluation." In *Sourcebook for Bibliographic Instruction*, ed. Katherine Branch, 45–57. Chicago, IL: Association of College and Research Libraries/American Library Association, 1993.

Beaubien, Anne K., Sharon A. Hogan, and Mary W. George. *Learning the Library: Concepts and Methods for Effective Bibliographic Instruction*. New York: R. R. Bowker Company, 1982.

Buschman, John. "Building Campus-wide Information Literacy Programs." Unpublished conference presentation, LOEX 2007. San Diego, CA, 2007.

Middle States Commission on Higher Education. *Developing Research & Communication Skills: Guidelines for Information Literacy in the Curriculum*. Philadelphia, PA: Middle States Commission on Higher Education, 2003.

Warner, Dorothy. "Programmatic Assessment of Information Literacy Skills using Rubrics." *Journal on Excellence in College Teaching* (in press).

Warner, Dorothy Anne. "Programmatic Assessment: Turning Process into Practice by Teaching for Learning." *The Journal of Academic Librarianship* 29(3) (2003): 169–176.

ADDITIONAL READINGS

Baker, Betsy. "Bibliographic Instruction: Building the Librarian/Faculty Partnership." *Reference Librarian* 24 (1989): 311–328.

Beck, Susan E., and Kate Manuel. "Folding Information Literacy into the General Education Mix: Recipes for Getting Started." In *Integrating Information Literacy into the College Experience*, eds. Julia K. Nims, Randal Baier, Rita Bullard, and Eric Owen, 11–16. Ann Arbor, MI: Pierian Press, 2003.

Berkowitz, Robert E. "Evaluating Student Performance: Information Skills Instruction and Assessment." *School Library Media Activities Monthly* 14 (October 1997): 23–27.

Black, Christine, Sarah Crest, and Mary Volland. "Building a Successful Information Literacy Infrastructure on the Foundation of Librarian-Faculty Collaboration." *Research Strategies* 18 (2001): 215–225.

Blandy, Susan Griswold. "The Librarians' Role in Academic Assessment and Accreditation: A Case Study." *The Reference Librarian* 38 (1992): 69–87.

Bober, Christopher, Sonia Poulin, and Luigina Vileno. "Evaluating Library Instruction in Academic Libraries: A Critical Review of the Literature, 1980–1993." *The Reference Librarian* 51/52 (1995): 53–71.

Chapman, Julie M. "The Portfolio: An Instruction Program Assessment Tool." *Reference Services Review* 29(4) (2001): 294–300.

Clarke, Kathy, and Rebecca Feind. "The Role of a Competency Test in Supporting and Promoting the Integration of Information Literacy in the Undergraduate Curriculum at James Madison University." In *Integrating Information Literacy into the College Experience*, eds. Julia K. Nim, Randal Baier, Rita Bullard, and Eric Owen, 61–67. Ann Arbor, MI: Pierian Press, 2003.

Coupe, Jill. "Undergraduate Library Skills: Two Surveys at Johns Hopkins University." *Research Strategies* 11(4) (1993): 188–201.

DeVault, Esme, Amanda Gluibizzi, and Ann Glannon, "Bringing 'Law and Order' into the Library: Evidence-Based Inquiry in Information Literacy Instruction at the Wheelock College Library." In *Integrating Information Literacy into the College Experience*, eds. Julia K. Nim, Randal Baier, Rita Bullard, and Eric Owen, 49–59. Ann Arbor, MI: Pierian Press, 2003.

Ducas, Ada M., and Nicole Michaud-Oystryk. "Toward a New Enterprise: Capitalizing on the Faculty/Librarian Partnership." *College & Research Libraries* 64(1) (January 2003): 55–74.

Dugan, Robert E., and Peter Hernon. "Outcomes Assessment: Not Synonymous with Inputs and Outputs." *The Journal of Academic Librarianship* 28(6) (November 2002): 376–380.

Dunn, Kathleen. "Assessing Information Literacy Skills in the California State University: A Progress Report." *The Journal of Academic Librarianship* 28(1) (January-March 2002): 26–35.

Dusenbury, Carolyn, Monica Fusich, Kathleen Kenny, and Beth Woodard. *Read This First: An Owner's Guide to the New Model Statement of Objectives for Academic Bibliographic Instruction*. Chicago, IL: Association of College and Research Libraries, 1991.

Fagan, Jody Condit. "How to Know What You Want Them to Know: Rediscovering Objectives by Reviewing Evaluative Materials." *Research Strategies* 18 (2001): 75–83.

Fain, Margaret, Peggy Bates, and Robert Stevens. "Promoting Collaboration with Faculty." In *Integrating Information Literacy into the College Experience*, eds. Julia K. Nim, Randal Baier, Rita Bullard, and Eric Owen, 205–211. Ann Arbor, MI: Pierian Press, 2003.

Fast, Margaret, and Jeanne Armstrong. "The Course Portfolio in a Library Setting." *Research Strategies* 19 (2003): 4–56.

Feinberg, Richard, and Christine King. "Performance Evaluation in Bibliographic Instruction Workshop Courses: Assessing What Students Do as a Measure of What They Know." *Reference Services Review* 20(2) (Summer 1992): 75–80.

Fitz-Gibbon, Carol Taylor, and Lynn Lyons Morris. *How to Design a Program Evaluation*. Newbury Park, CA: Sage Publications, 1987.

Flaspohler, Molly R. "Information Literacy Program Assessment: One Small College takes the Big Plunge." *Reference Services Review* 31(2) (2003): 129–140.

Fourie, Ina, and Daleen van Niekerk. "Using Portfolio Assessment in a Module in Research Information Skills." *Education for Information* 17(4) (December 1999): 333–352.

Gaff, Jerry G., and James L. Ratcliff. *Handbook of the Undergraduate Curriculum: A Comprehensive Guide to Purposes, Structures, Practices, and Change*. San Francisco, CA: Jossey-Bass, 1997.

Gilchrist, Debra. "Collaborative Teaching through Inquiry-Based Instruction." In *What is Good Instruction Now? Library Instruction for the 90s*, ed. Linda Shirato, 51–56. Ann Arbor, MI: Pierian Press, 1993.

Greer, Arlene, Lee Weston, and Mary Alm. "Assessment of Learning Outcomes: A Measure of Progress in Library Literacy." *College & Research Libraries* 52 (November 1991): 549–557.

Hopkins, Frances L. "Bibliographic Instruction as a Liberal Art: An Application of Patrick Wilson's Theory of Pragmatic Bibliography." In *Back to the Books: Bibliographic Instruction and the Theory of Information Sources*, ed. Ross Atkinson, 15–29. Chicago, IL: Association of Research Libraries, American Library Association, 1983.

Iannuzzi, Patricia. "Faculty Development and Information Literacy: Establishing Campus Partnerships." *Reference Services Review* 26(3/4) (Fall/Winter 1998): 97–116.

Jackson, Shaun, Carol Hansen, and Lauren Fowler. "Using Selected Assessment Data to Inform Information Literacy Program Planning with Campus Partners." *Research Strategies* 20 (2005): 44–56.

Jenkins, Jim, and Marcia Boosinger. "Collaborating with Campus Administrators and Faculty to Integrate Information Literacy and Assessment into the Core Curriculum." *The Southeastern Librarian* 50(4) (Winter 2003): 26–31.

Johnson, Corey M., Sarah K. McCord, and Scott Walter. "Instructional Outreach Across the Curriculum: Enhancing the Liaison Role at a Research University." *The Reference Librarian* 82 (2003): 19–37.

Junn, Ellen, Suellen Cox, Patricia Szeszulski, and Sorel Reisman. "The CSU Fullerton Initiative: Integrating Information Competence into the Curriculum." In *Integrating Information Literacy into the College Experience*, eds. Julia K. Nim, Randal Baier, Rita Bullard, and Eric Owen, 107–115. Ann Arbor, MI: Pierian Press, 2003.

King-Blandford, Marcia. "The Quest to Understand K-16 Information Literacy Skills." In *Integrating Information Literacy into the College Experience*, eds. Julia K. Nim, Randal Baier, Rita Bullard, and Eric Owen, 145–151. Ann Arbor, MI: Pierian Press, 2003.

"King's College Takes a Multitiered Approach to Information Literacy Assessment." *AAC&U News* (January/February 2005).

Knight, Lorrie. "The Role of Assessment in Library User Education." *Reference Services Review* 30(1) (2002): 15–24.

Kobelski, Pamela, and Mary Reichel. "Conceptual Frameworks for Bibliographic Instruction." *The Journal of Academic Librarianship* 7(2) (May 1981): 73–77.

Kunkel, Lilith R., Susan M. Weaver, and Kim N. Cook. "What Do They Know? An Assessment of Undergraduate Library Skills." *The Journal of Academic Librarianship* (November 1996): 430–434.

Landrum, R. Eric, and Diana M. Muench. "Assessing Students' Library Skills and Knowledge: The Library Research Strategies Questionnaire." *Psychological Reports* 75 (1994): 1619–1628.

Lawson, Mollie D. "Assessment of a College Freshman Course in Information Resources." *Library Review* 48(2) (1999): 73–78.

Lindauaer, Bonnie Gratch. "Defining and Measuring the Library's Impact on Campuswide Outcomes." *College & Research Libraries* 59(6) (November 1998): 546–70.

Loacker, Georgine. "Designing a National Assessment System: Alverno's Institutional Perspective." Paper commissioned by the U.S. Office of Education, National Center for Education Statistics, in response to the National Education Goals Panel: America 2000: An Education Strategy. Washington, DC, November 1991.

Lorenzen, Michael. "A Brief History of Library Information in the United States of America." *Illinois Libraries* 83(2) (Spring 2001): 8–18.

Mackey, Thomas P., and Trudi E. Jacobson. "Integrating Information Literacy in Lower-and Upper-Level Courses: Developing Scalable Models for Higher Education." *JGE: The Journal of General Education* 53(3–4) (2004): 201–224.

Maki, Peggy. "Developing an Assessment Plan to Learn about Student Learning." *The Journal of Academic Librarianship* 28(1) (January–March 2002): 8–13.

Meulemans, Yvonne Nalani. "Assessment City: The Past, Present, and Future State of Information Literacy Assessment." *College & Undergraduate Libraries* 9(2) (2002): 61–74.

Middle States Commission on Higher Education. *Developing Research & Communication Skills: Guidelines for Information Literacy in the Curriculum*. Philadelphia, PA: Middle States Commission on Higher Education, 2003.

Middle States Commission on Higher Education. *Student Learning Assessment: Options and Resources*. Philadelphia, PA: Middle States Commission on Higher Education, 2003.

Mulherrin, Elizabeth, "Teaching Information Literacy Skills to Undergraduates: The Electronic Research Log Model." In *Integrating Information Literacy into the College Experience*, eds. Julia K. Nim, Randal Baier, Rita Bullard, and Eric Owen, 183–186. Ann Arbor, MI: Pierian Press, 2003.

Nahl-Jakobovits, Diane, and Leon A. Jakobovits. "Learning Principles and the Library Environment." *Research Strategies* 8(2) (1990): 74–81.

———. "Bibliographic Instructional Design for Information Literacy: Integrating Affective and Cognitive Objectives." *Research Strategies* 11(2) (Spring 1993): 73–88.

O'Connor, Lisa G., Carolyn J. Radcliff, and Julie A. Gedeon. "Assessing Information Literacy Skills: Developing a Standardized Instrument for Institutional and Longitudinal Measurement." Proceedings of the Tenth National Conference of the Association of College and Research Libraries. Chicago, IL: Association of College and Research Libraries, 2001.

————. "Applying Systems Design and Item Response Theory to the Problem of Measuring Information Literacy Skills." College & Research Libraries 63(6) (November 2002): 528–543.

Palomba, Catherine A., and Trudy W. Banta. Assessment Essentials: Planning, Implementing, and Improving Assessment in Higher Education. San Francisco, CA: Jossey-Bass, 1999.

Pausch, Lois M., and Mary Pagliero Popp. "Assessment of Information Literacy: Lessons from the Higher Education Movement." Paper presented at the Eighth Annual Conference of the Association of College and Research Libraries, 1997. http://www.ala.org/ala/acrlbucket/nashville1997pap/pauschpopp.cfm (accessed March 7, 2008).

Perrault, Anna H., Vicki L. Gregory, and James O. Carey. "The Integration of Assessment of Student Learning Outcomes with Teaching Effectiveness." Journal of Education for Library and Information Science 43(4) (Fall 2002): 270–282.

Rabine, Julie, and Catherine Cardwell. "Start Making Sense: Practical Approaches to Outcomes Assessment for Libraries." Research Strategies 17(4) (2000): 319–335.

Ragains, Patrick. "Evaluation of Academic Librarians' Instructional Performance: Report of a National Survey." Research Strategies 15(3) (1997): 159–175.

Reichel, Mary, and Mary Ann Ramey, eds. Conceptual Frameworks for Bibliographic Education: Theory into Practice. Littleton, CO: Libraries Unlimited, Inc., 1987.

Rockman, Ilene F. "Editorial: The Importance of Assessment." Reference Services Review 30(3) (2002): 181–182.

————. "Strengthening Connections Between Information Literacy, General Education, and Assessment Efforts." Library Trends 51(2) (Fall 2002): 185–198.

Rockman, Ilene F., Delores Nasom McBroome, Marlowe Berg, and Maria Grant. "A System-Wide Multi-Campus Approach to Integrating Information Competence into the Learning Outcomes of Academic Departments in the California State University System." In Integrating Information Literacy into the College Experience, eds. Julia K. Nim, Randal Baier, Rita Bullard, and Eric Owen, 29–32. Ann Arbor, MI: Pierian Press, 2003.

Selegean, John Cornell, Martha Lou Thomas, and Marie Louise Richman. "Long-Range Effectiveness of Library Use Instruction." College & Research Libraries 44 (November 1983): 476–480.

Simmons, Howard L. "Information Literacy and Accreditation: A Middle States Association Perspective." In New Directions for Higher Education: No. 78. Information Literacy: Developing Students as Independent Learners, eds. D. W. Farmer and Terrence F. Mech, 15–25. San Francisco: Jossey-Bass Publishers, 1992.

Snavely, Loanne L., and Carol A. Wright. "Research Portfolio Use in Undergraduate Honors Education: Assessment Tool and Model for Future Work." The Journal of Academic Librarianship 29(5) (September 2003): 298–303.

Sonntag, Gabriela, and Donna M. Ohr. "The Development of a Lower-Division, General Education, Course-Integrated Information Literacy Program." College & Research Libraries 57 (July 1996): 331–338.

Sugarman, Tammy S., and Laura G. Burtle. "From 50 Minutes to 15 Weeks: Teaching a Semester-Long Information Literacy Course within a Freshman Learning Community." In Integrating Information Literacy into the College Experience, eds. Julia K. Nim, Randal Baier, Rita Bullard, and Eric Owen, 187–198. Ann Arbor, MI: Pierian Press, 2003.

Thompson, Gary B. "Information Literacy Accreditation Mandates: What They Mean for Faculty and Librarians." Library Trends 51(2) (Fall 2002): 218–241.

Thompson, Helen M., and Susan A. Henley. *Fostering Information Literacy: Connecting National Standards, Goals 2000, and the SCANS Report*. Englewood, CO: Libraries Unlimited, Inc., 2000.

Tiefel, Virginia. "Evaluating a Library User Education Program: A Decade of Experience." *College & Research Libraries* 50 (March 1989): 249–259.

Wiggins, Grant, and Jay McTighe. *Understanding by Design*. Alexandria, VA: Association for Supervision and Curriculum Development, 2005.

Williams, Janet L. "Creativity in Assessment of Library Instruction." *Reference Services Review* 28(4) (2000): 323–334.

Young, James B., and Ashley Taliaferro Williams. "The Integration of Information Literacy Skills in a Year-Long Learning Community Program: A Faculty and Librarian Collaboration." In *Integrating Information Literacy into the College Experience*, eds. Julia K. Nim, Randal Baier, Rita Bullard, and Eric Owen, 19–24. Ann Arbor, MI: Pierian Press, 2003.

Young, Rosemary M., and Stephena Harmony. *Working with Faculty to Design Undergraduate Information Literacy Programs: A How-to-do-it Manual for Librarians*. New York: Neal-Schuman Publishers, Inc., 1999.

Young, Sheila, and Julia C. Blixrud. "Research Library Involvement in Learning Outcomes Assessment Programs." *ARL* 230/231 (October/December 2003): 14–17.

2

Evaluation as Inherent in Information Literacy

Consider the cognitive process that you expect the students to develop between the freshman and the senior years. The framework presented for this purpose has been adapted from the cognitive taxonomy developed by Benjamin Bloom (1956). This adapted framework is used to define the sequential cognitive expectations of students developing their information literacy skills. The adaptation is rooted in Eisenberg's and Berkowitz's work (1988) which applied Bloom's Taxonomy of Cognitive Objectives to their "Big Six Skills" K-12 information skills curriculum. They matched the cognitive levels defined by Bloom to information-related behaviors (see Figure 2.1).

The framework presented here applies the cognitive levels of the taxonomy to the learning objectives developed for each discipline. For example, two objectives for the sociology proposal represent skills that are achieved at different cognitive levels. The first skill requires evidence of the student first identifying the need (knowledge level), describing the problem that requires the need (comprehension level), and then actually demonstrating (i.e., applying the skill to a problem solving situation) utilization of a government source to solve the information need (application level). The sociology objective expects that *students will understand how government information is organized and identify the need to access information from municipal, state, federal, or international government sources, including utilizing the Congressional Research Service and U.S. Census Bureau publications.*

At the next cognitive level of analysis, "students discover an idea's characteristics by breaking down an idea into its parts and discovering relationships. Analyzing content to find causes, conclusions, or supporting evidence is indicative of the analysis level" (Eisenberg and Berkowitz, 1988, 102). The objective that follows requires the student to analyze the selected resources, determine what is additionally needed, and seek information from the appropriate disciplinary source. It then requires the student to achieve the cognitive level of synthesis. Eisenberg and Berkowitz describe the cognitive level

COGNITIVE LEVEL	INFORMATION ORIENTED ACTION—ABILITY TO:
Knowledge	Repeat appropriate information (with or without comprehension)
Comprehension	Demonstrate understanding of information (e.g., translate/interpret/extrapolate)
Application	Transform information to find solutions to problems
Analysis	Break information down into its parts/discover unique characteristics
Synthesis	Combine information in order to uncover & develop relationships (e.g., hypothesize)
Evaluation	Make appraisals/judgments about information based on either external or internal standards

Figure 2.1 Bloom's Cognitive Levels and Associated Information Oriented Actions. *Source:* Eisenberg and Berkowitz 1988, 102. Reprinted with permission.

of synthesis as "the ability to integrate information drawn from a range of sources. Synthesis brings together existing information and adds value to it by restructuring and repackaging the information to meet defined tasks" (Eisenberg and Berkowitz, 1988, 116). The sociology objective expects that *students will recognize the interdisciplinary nature of sociology and identify the need for seeking information from other disciplines to support their research. In order to do this, students will distinguish between and appropriately use standard sociology sources and those sources outside of the profession.*

The evaluation level will be one that is achieved at different stages for different disciplines (e.g., in the film studies illustration [Chapter 3], the evaluation skill begins intensively at the introductory level and is developed throughout the course sequence). Selected objectives in the other proposals have been identified as having such "graduated," or progressive, cognitive level(s). By this, it is meant that the skill will be introduced early in the college career and built upon so that the skill is mastered at the evaluation level by the senior year. An example of this is included in several of the sequences requiring that *students will judge the value of a resource by noting its reliability, validity, accuracy, authority, timeliness, point of view or bias* (a graduated skill developed throughout the sequence from the cognitive levels of knowledge to evaluation). This objective is intended to corelate to the following, upper-level objective expecting that *students will be able to compare/contrast and critically evaluate information from multiple sources in order to ensure the accuracy of the information used* (achieving the cognitive levels of analysis, synthesis, and evaluation). Although we begin to introduce students to the differences in source type and source content at the freshman level, this objective is not assessed until the upper levels of the discipline after students have practiced the skill and when the requirement exists to describe the process of comparing and contrasting information from multiple sources. D'Angelo (2001) provides an excellent example of an assignment in an upper-level business course that requires analysis of the text of a variety of source types. The content must be evaluated for its relevance, credibility, and validity.

Evaluation is inherent in everything we teach. At the introductory stage, the student asks, which source type do I need? Which will work best for my particular question? In the days before the World Wide Web, we introduced and showed the students various print sources to identify the differences in content and quality. We compared coverage of topics in a local popular newspaper vs. the *New York Times*, identified the content and coverage in a news magazine (a general audience publication) vs. the coverage and content in a scholarly journal (written for a specific disciplinary audience). We identified how the physical object contributes to our understanding of its content. If we consider two objects, for example, a scholarly encyclopedia volume vs. a popular/commercial title, one knows instantly that there is a difference in the approach to the work and that the content will be different. This is also instantly clear when comparing the physical volumes of a general audience news magazine to a scholarly journal. "All literature units exhibit the basic properties of object, i.e., the constituting device O; content, i.e., the knowledge expressed to be recorded, stored, displayed, and transmitted C; and a use potential U. O-C-U are correlative terms which hold true for any human literature, at any given point in time" (Rawski, 1983, 34).

For those of us who were educated before the Web generation, this physical object plays a big role in our ability to evaluate information. Print literacy is at the basis of information literacy and to our understanding of knowledge production from data to information to knowledge.

In the era of the World Wide Web, information is now seen primarily through the lens of the online environment and often separated from its original context (e.g., an isolated article discovered using *Google Scholar* has been separated from the context of the journal that it appeared in). The pre-Web generation knows more easily what the context is of an electronic source and cannot take for granted that the students understand that. When students see an article that is in *JSTOR* or *Project Muse*, they may have no idea where they "are" (some students think that *JSTOR* and *Project Muse* are the names of journals)—they're seeing an article on the screen that looks the same to them as something that they've identified on a "free" Web site. It all has the same look and the context is unclear.

The typical college freshman comes to us with a deficit in the research experience and requires a firm grounding in "the basics" before she or he can be expected to conduct the level of source analysis described by D'Angelo or Hynd-Shanahan (ahead). This was also the case in the pre-Web environment.

Several comments by freshmen, in response to an assessment question about the reliability of information found at a Web site, illustrate the need to establish an introductory grounding in source evaluation. One student "knew the information was current because some of the articles had dates" and another found Google.com to be "pretty reliable" and AskJeeves.com to be "not as reliable as Google." Another "knew the information on the site was reliable because it had a short html Web address and it was very thorough in writing and information." Another stated that .edu or .org domains "were reliable because .edu and .org are most known." Another found "free" Web sites "to be the easiest to access and they also provided [the student] with the most recent, accurate information" (Warner, in press).

From comments like these came the recognition that students need to first utilize academic resources in order to recognize and understand what quality *is* before they can identify "quality" on the "free" Web. Students need to be exposed to experiences that will teach them "context." Discussion of the peer review process needs to include the recognition of the author's credentials. The context that the peer reviewed journals falls within needs to be explained. This may require a visualization of the peer-reviewed journal in contrast to a news magazine. Are not these evaluative skills rooted in the print culture? A reference to *Newsweek* prompts a visual image of the print news magazine. What do students "see" when we use the term, "database"? There needs to be deliberate teaching of source and content evaluation so that students recognize and understand the object, the content within the object, and the purpose or potential use of that content. In other words, the student needs to match the information need with the appropriate source type and know when to appropriately select a scholarly encyclopedia, a book, an article, or a government agency Web site to fill the information need.

Typically undertaken in a general education sequence or a research writing course, the level of the evaluation process that freshmen need to master includes identifying the differences between the object, content, and purpose of several source types. Scholarly subject encyclopedias provide background information for an initial overview of a topic and often provide a bibliography. Books also provide background information and a more thorough overview of the topic than an article, but the information may be dated. The difference between the "free" Web and subscription databases can be described by the quality check of the peer-review publication process and the organization provided by indexing. Subscription databases contain information that can be intended for a general/interdisciplinary audience or a discipline-specific audience. The information need should determine the selection of the appropriate database.

Bibliographic instruction is the method to teach students how to locate information by learning and using the bibliography of the discipline and the bibliographic systems of control (i.e., classification, relevant indexing terms). While the terminology for our bibliographic curriculum's purpose has slowly and steadily morphed into "information literacy" as technologies have multiplied both the technical methods of retrieval (online catalogs, for instance) and then sources and formats of information to retrieve in an ever-wider variety of "texts" of all sorts, the process is still rooted in the bibliography of the discipline.

Information literacy and the many and various literacies largely rely on a fundamental enabling concept within literacy itself: critical distance and reflexive evaluation. This concept itself is so deeply embedded within literacy that its very existence came about because of literacy. Goody and Watt (1977, 469–470) provide an explanation:

[H]uman intercourse was . . . no longer restricted to the impermanency of oral converse. . . . [I]t was only when the simplicity and flexibility of later alphabetic writing made widespread literacy possible that for the first time there began to take concrete shape . . . a society that was essentially literate. . . . In oral societies the cultural tradition is transmitted almost entirely by face-to-face communication; and changes in its content are accompanied by the homeostatic process of forgetting or transforming those parts . . . that cease to be either necessary or relevant. Literate societies . . . are faced with permanently recorded versions of the past and its beliefs; and because the past is thus set apart from the present, historical enquiry becomes possible. This in turn encourages skepticism . . . not only about the legendary past, but about received ideas [through the process of] recording of verbal statements and then . . . the dissecting of them.

In the more mature phases of information literacy, history students are to engage in three unique processes: "sourcing (an evaluation of the source of information), contextualization (placing the text's arguments in a particular time period and context), and corroboration (looking for corroborative evidence across different sources)" (Hynd-Shanahan, Holschuh, and Hubbard, 2004, 142). Competencies for literature students include social-practice concepts such as understanding "the authorship, production, dissemination, or availability of literary production" (ALA/ACRL, 2007) and "an understanding of texts" (NCTE/IRA, 2008) and stress "demonstrat[ing] critical thinking in the research process" and "understand[ing] the relationship between received knowledge and the production of new knowledge . . ." (ALA/ACRL, 2007). Science students must recognize the relationships among "primary, secondary, and tertiary sources [and that they] vary in importance and use with each discipline." The goal is that the student "critically evaluates the procured information and its sources" (ALA, 2006). Each and every one of these conceptions comes to define being information literate in critical-reflexive terms (Buschman, under review) at a stage that we hope our students will mature into over their college experience.

REFERENCES

American Library Association (ALA), Association of College and Research Libraries (ACRL), Literatures in English Section (2007). *Research Competency Guidelines for Literatures in English*. http://www.ala.org/ala/acrl/acrlstandards/researchcompetenciesles.cfm (accessed March 13, 2008).

American Library Association (ALA), Association of College and Research Libraries (ACRL), STS Task Force on Information Literacy for Science and Technology (2006). *Information Literacy Standards for Science and Engineering/Technology*. http://www.ala.org/ala/acrl/acrlstandards/infolitscitech.cfm (accessed March 13, 2008).

Bloom, Benjamin S., ed., Max D. Engelhart, Edward J. Furst, Walker H. Hill, David R. Krathwohl. *Taxonomy of Educational Objectives: The Classification of Educational Goals: Handbook I: Cognitive Domain*. New York: McKay, 1956.

Buschman, John. "Information Literacy, 'New' Literacies, and Literacy" (under review).

D'Angelo, Barbara J. "Using Source Analysis to Promote Critical Thinking." *Research Strategies* 18 (2001): 303–309.

Eisenberg, Michael B.and Berkowitz, Robert E. *Curriculum Initiative: An Agenda and Strategy for Library Media Programs*. Norwood, NJ: Ablex Publishing, 1988.

Goody, Jack and Watt, Ian. "The Consequences of Literacy." In *Power and Ideology in Education*, eds. Jerome Karabel and A. H. Halsey, 456–473. New York: Oxford University Press, 1977.

Hynd-Shanahan, Cynthia, Jodi Patrick Holschuh, and Betty P. Hubbard. "Thinking Like a Historian: Students' Reading of Multiple Historical Documents." *Journal of Literacy Research* 36(2) (2004), 141–176.

National Council of Teachers of English and the International Reading Association (NCTE/IRA). *Standards for the English Language Arts* (2008). http://www.ncte.org/about/over/standards/110846.htm (accessed October 3, 2007).

Rawski, Conrad H. "On the Nature of Literatures: A Synergetic Attempt." In *Back to the Books: Bibliographic Instruction and the Theory of Information Sources*. Papers Presented at the 101st Annual Conference of the American Library Association, ed. Ross Atkinson, 31–56. Chicago, IL: Association of College and Research Libraries, American Library Association, 1983.

Warner, Dorothy. "Programmatic Assessment of Information Literacy Skills Using Rubrics." *Journal on Excellence in College Teaching* (in press).

ADDITIONAL READINGS

Britt, M. Anne, and Cindy Aglinskas. "Improving Students' Ability to Identify and Use Source Information." *Cognition and Instruction* 20(4) (2002): 485–522.

D'Angelo, Barbara J. "Using Source Analysis to Promote Critical Thinking." *Research Strategies* 18(4) (2001): 303–309.

Rouet, Jean-Francois, M. Anne Britt, Robert A. Mason, and Charles A. Perfetti. "Using Multiple Sources of Evidence to Reason about History." *Journal of Educational Psychology* 88(3) (1996): 478–493.

Rouet, Jean-Francois, Monik Favart, M. Anne Britt, and Charles A. Perfetti. "Studying and Using Multiple Documents in History: Effects of Discipline Expertise." *Cognition and Instruction* 15(1) (1997): 85–106.

Schaus, Margaret. "Hands-on History." *C&RL News* 9 (October 1990): 825–831.

Widder, Agnes Haigh, and John Coogan. "Who was Berut? Using Correspondence between World Statesmen in Bibliographic Instruction." *Research Strategies* 5 (Summer 1987): 135–138.

Wineburg, Samuel S. "Historical Problem Solving: A Study of the Cognitive Processes Used in the Evaluation of Documentary and Pictorial Evidence." *Journal of Educational Psychology* 83(1) (1991): 73–87.

3

Recommended Sequence for Bibliographic and Information Literacy for a New Program: Film Studies

GOALS AND OBJECTIVES OF THE FILM STUDIES CURRICULUM

The curriculum of the study of film will depend upon the discipline within which it is based. An emphasis on either film production or film criticism may exist if situated in a communication department, while a combination of literary and film analysis, including intertextual analysis, will exist if situated in an English Department. Or, an interdisciplinary approach may involve the participation of multiple departments in the development of the film studies curriculum. An interdisciplinary approach could involve the participation of art history, business, history, political science, American studies, fine arts, psychology, or sociology departments in addition to communication and English departments. Thus, the specific curriculum will influence the collection needs and the bibliographic and information literacy objectives taught.

Before determining the specific information literacy objectives, the goals and objectives of the specific film studies curricula must be examined. While certainly not exhausting the possibilities, the following are potential curricular goals and objectives for film production, film analysis, literary analysis, and intertextuality. These provide a glimpse into the complexity of collection support and information literacy requirements needed for the multiple approaches to this field.

The development of information literacy objectives for one's particular academic setting will be dependent upon the institutional approach taken to film studies. Students developing the skills inherent in film production will need to comprehend and apply the filmmaking techniques of narrative filmmaking (script writing, cinematography, editing, directing, sound). Students developing the skill of film analysis will need to identify and apply an understanding of vocabulary in the field; identify, define, and analyze the elements of film form; identify, define, and analyze basic elements of filmmaking techniques in both narrative and non-narrative cinema; identify, define, and analyze structural patterns in film; and identify and define patterns that characterize the work of specific film directors. Students developing the skill of literary analysis will need to identify and apply various modes of literary criticism, including formal, structural, psychological, and sociological methods of analysis. Students examining film history will need to recognize and apply an understanding of the international context that has shaped films, including the historical, political, and cultural influences on the development of film; identify and define movements in film history (including early cinema, classical Hollywood cinema, non-narrative forms: documentary and experimental, alternatives to Hollywood form, The New Hollywood, contemporary alternatives to Hollywood, the future of cinema, specific film genres from classic through revisionist periods); identify and define the technical and aesthetic development of film; recognize the characteristics of major national cinemas; evaluate the influence of one's work on others, including the role of specific film directors; and apply an understanding of the development and influence of film institutions and industry practices. Students examining literary history will need to apply an understanding of the characteristics of literary movements; and apply an understanding of the cultural and historical contexts of literary works. Students studying film theory will need to evaluate formalist, structural, and ideological theories and their application to specific films; and analyze the ways in which film positions the viewer. Students developing the critical tools needed to examine the intertextual influence of film will need to identify and define the key formal elements that characterize both film and literary genres; and analyze forms of intertextuality operating within selected film adaptations. The curricular objectives here were primarily developed from the adapted program and course proposals for the Film Studies Concentration for the English major at Rider University (written by Dr. Cynthia A. Lucia, with Dr. Roberta Clipper Sethi, Chairperson, Department of English 2004–2007, reprinted with permission from Rider University) and from course descriptions in the Rider University *Undergraduate Catalog 06/07*. Course descriptions in the undergraduate catalogs for the Film Studies major at Keene State University (2006) and the Communication Studies major at Plymouth State University (2006) were also consulted.

Included in the "skeleton" curriculum map ahead (Figure 3.1) are examples of potential course requirements and selected electives for the study of film. The complexity of the curriculum will depend upon the degree of interdisciplinary influences that may exist within the curriculum. The focus of study (e.g., on production, film criticism, etc.) will determine which courses will be identified as requirements for the major. The curriculum map for film studies is an illustration for a new program for which information literacy instruction has not yet taken place. The elements to be included in the map will include whether information literacy is identified in the course syllabus, whether an instructional opportunity exists, the professor(s) to be contacted, and the information literacy objectives to be taught in each course.

INFORMATION LITERACY OBJECTIVES
AND BIBLIOGRAPHIC OUTLINE

The concentration or major would begin during the sophomore year. This assumes that students (as freshmen) would have begun the process of source evaluation in their general education requirements (e.g., Research Writing) by learning the differences between the object, content, and purpose of various source types. In order to pursue their

COURSE SEQUENCE (Requirements will be dependent upon the focus of study)	Information Literacy in Syllabi or Catalog (or Opportunity)	Information Literacy Objectives	Professors (scheduled for upcoming Academic Year)
Introductory Level			
Film Production I			
Film Analysis			
Literary Analysis			
Film History			
Literary History			
Documentary Film and Video			
Intermediate Level			
Film Production II			
Intermediate Production Studio			
Literature Seminars (e.g., choice of study of the novel, drama, poem, short fiction)			
Literature Seminars (e.g., choice of Shakespeare; Victorian; 19th, 20th, or contemporary American or British, Black & Multiethnic literature)			
Film Genres			
Film Theory			
Film Directors			
Scriptwriting			
National Cinema			
Literature and Film			
Theater and Film			
Psychology and Film			
Film Music			
Alfred Hitchcock			
Political Film			
Film as Popular Culture			
Sex and Cinema in the 20th Century (and beyond)			
Advanced Level			
Film Production III & IV			
Advanced Production Techniques			
Film Adaptation			
Film and Identity Politics			
Seminar			
Senior Research Project			

Figure 3.1 Preliminary Curriculum Map for Film Studies.

research in the introductory level film studies courses, students will need to be proficient in several areas, beginning with their knowledge of the literature for the major.

All of the information literacy objectives will be introduced at the introductory level and students will be expected to progress in each skill to the evaluation level by the conclusion of the major. Sources referenced for these learning objectives include the *Research Competency Guidelines for Literatures in English* (ALA, 2007) and the bibliographic guide by Emmons (2006).

In order to **understand the structure of information within the field of film studies (which may include literary studies) research** (Goal 1), *students will differentiate between primary, secondary, and tertiary sources* (Objective A), and *students will distinguish among the purposes of different types of sources* (Objective B), (both objectives learned as a graduated skill development with the expectation of reaching the analysis level at the introductory level of the film studies curriculum). The examples of primary, secondary, and tertiary sources that follow concentrate on film production, analysis, history, theory, and the intertextual influence of film. Source types and specific references for literary analysis, theory, and history may be identified by using the search process described in Chapter 1. A contribution of note to the film sources listed ahead was the proposal by Pence et al. (2003).

Primary sources include celluloid prints, screenplays, fan Web sites, film industry Web sites, relevant Web sites including Gateways (e.g., *The Black Film Center & Archive, The Internet Movie Database*), Web sites of professional associations (e.g., the *American Film Institute, British Film Institute, Motion Picture Association of America [MPAA]*), scripts, autobiographies, archived materials in museums (including specific museums of film as well as museums with significant film collections) and archives (e.g., studio, format, content-based and national library collections), and other organizations/associations (professional organizations of technicians, preservationists, scholars, and historians).

Secondary sources are those sources written for both the general audience as well as the critics and scholars. They include popular and critical reaction to film, including reviews and critical scholarship. These may appear in the format of textbooks, monographs, anthologies, articles in general interest magazines and newspapers, articles in specialized/critical film journals (*American Cinematographer, Cineaste, Frauen und Film*), articles in film review sources (*New York Times, Variety*), and conference papers. Also included in this category are biographies (e.g., filmmakers: actors, art directors, cinematographers, costume designers, directors, editors, writers) and film adaptations. *Hybrids* of these formats appear in the form of encyclopedias, histories (e.g., production histories), and plot summaries.

Tertiary sources are those sources produced by bibliographers, indexers, or publishers that appear in the form of fact and finding tools. *Finding tools* include bibliographies either in single publications or library catalogs, indexes, and abstracts. *Fact tools* include handbooks, dictionaries, directories (e.g., film festivals and awards), performance schedules (including festival and television scheduling), and biographical sets. *Guides* include guides to film literature (filmographies), biographical guides, and guides to reference books. Sources for film, video and DVD (e.g., archives, images, rental outlets), Web sites for film venues, Newsgroup access (discussion groups on all topics of cinema), relevant Web sites including Gateways (e.g., *Greatest Films of All Time, TV Guide Online Movie Database*) are also tertiary sources.

In order to **identify and use research tools in film (literary, if relevant) studies that are used for specific purposes** (Goal 2), *students will effectively use library catalogs to identify relevant collections in libraries and archives* (Objective C); *students will identify, distinguish and effectively utilize sources for reviews or criticism* (Objective D), *students will identify and effectively utilize indexing or abstracting services* (Objective E), *students will determine the most appropriate source(s) for the information need by evaluative selection from among multiple source types* (Objective F) (all objectives to be learned as a graduated skill development with the expectation of reaching the analysis level at the introductory level of the course sequence).

In order to **understand the technical and ethical issues involved in the use of sources** (Goal 3), *students will appropriately acknowledge their sources according to the required bibliographical format, including appropriately acknowledging quotations, accurately quoting, paraphrasing, and avoiding plagiarism* (Objective G) (the application level will be reached at the introductory level of the course sequence and maintained throughout the sequence).

RECOMMENDATIONS FOR TEACHING AND ASSESSING INFORMATION LITERACY SKILLS

The bibliographic outline (above) will provide the basis of the film studies information literacy instruction in one of the required introductory courses. Students in the introductory-level instruction session will be introduced to the film information literacy objectives relevant to the focus of their curriculum. Students will be expected to demonstrate analytical skills at the introductory level of this program. They will proceed to the synthesis and evaluation levels in their intermediate- and advanced-level courses. Multiple assignments will require students to demonstrate their abilities to appropriately select information sources.

To determine the extent of the students' research process, an electronic research planner (Figure 3.2) will be completed to maintain a log of sources consulted in the process of conducting their research. Each planner will be archived at the library's Web site for continued use by the students for the duration of the major. These will be submitted to the film professor with each assignment together with a list of works cited. In the shared process of assessment, the professor will provide recommendations to the librarian(s) for skill reinforcement needed in the course-integrated instruction to take place in the intermediate-level courses.

At the advanced level, students will consult with the librarian(s) prior to beginning their senior project. Utilizing the research planner and a review of previously completed planners, students will prepare their course of research and receive recommendations from the librarian. Midway through the research process, the students will consult again

Information needed	Potential sources to fill the need	Was the information need met?	Was the source insufficient to meet the information need?

Figure 3.2 Research Planner.

with the librarian. During the consultation, the librarian and students will refer to the film information literacy objectives and mutually determine the extent of resource use and whether the "most appropriate sources for the information need" (Objective F) have been evaluated and then selected from among the multiple source types available. There will be an expectation, based upon the particular research project, that students appropriately select primary, secondary, and tertiary sources, and that they recognize that the intended purpose for each source is connected to their specific research question and need. The librarian and student will together identify the proficiency level reached for each objective. A rubric may be designed for this purpose (see Figure 10.5 for an example). The librarian will provide the film professor with the mutually determined assessment of the student's bibliographic and information literacy skills for consideration in the final grade on the senior project. To then determine the proficiency level in the aggregate, an average will be concluded from each of the mutually determined assessments of each objective. This summary will enable the librarians to recognize the objectives that require teaching and learning improvements. Thus, a process of continual enriching of the information literacy curriculum will be established.

REFERENCES

American Library Association (ALA), Association of College and Research Libraries (ACRL), Literatures in English Section (2007). *Research Competency Guidelines for Literatures in English*. http://www.ala.org/ala/acrl/acrlstandards/researchcompetenciesles.cfm (accessed March 13, 2008).

Emmons, Mark. *Film and Television: A Guide to the Reference Literature*. Westport, CT: Libraries Unlimited, 2006.

Keene State College. *Undergraduate and Graduate Catalog 2006–07*. Keene, NH: Keene State College, 2006.

Lucia, Cynthia A., with Roberta Clipper Sethi. *New Program Proposal and New Course Proposals for Film Studies Concentration*. Lawrenceville, NJ: Rider University, 2004–2007.

Pence, Jeffrey, Allison Gould, Albert Borroni, William Patrick Day, Elizabeth Hamilton, Jennifer Horne, and Geoff Pingree (2003). *Information Literacy Proposal: Cinema Studies Program*. http://collaborations.denison.edu/ohio5/grant/development/pence.html (accessed March 14, 2008).

Plymouth State University. *Academic Catalog 2006–2007*. Plymouth, NH: Plymouth State University, 2006.

Rider University. *Undergraduate Catalog 06/07*. Lawrenceville, NJ: Rider University, 2006.

4

An Illustration in Process: Recommended Sequence for Bibliographic and Information Literacy for an Interdisciplinary Program in the Sciences: The Integrated Sciences and Math Major

The integrated sciences and math (ISM) major, a new major housed in the Geological and Marine Sciences Department, utilizes faculty from the biology, chemistry, physics, and math departments. There is the additional relationship with faculty in the Teacher Preparation Department. Students who plan to teach science or math at the middle-school level must major in elementary education and select the middle school minor. The education students have a double major, and, in this case, that second major would be the ISM major.

The students in the major take an introductory course (100-level) and a capstone course (400-level) exclusively with students in their major. The catalog description for ISM–100, Introduction to the Integrated Sciences, describes the course as encouraging "students to begin asking questions and designing experiments to learn about the physical, life and earth sciences." The catalog description for ISM–410, Seminar in the Integrated Sciences, describes the course as covering science topics "that extend beyond the range of a single science discipline. Students will evaluate articles (from scientific journals, popular science magazines, newspapers, etc.) to discern the connections among various scientific disciplines, including mathematics. Specifically, students will present a written critique of the articles focusing on the proper use of the scientific method, the data analysis techniques (e.g., statistics, mathematics, etc.), and on the plausibility of the interpretations. Students will take turns leading the discussion of the articles. Students will also present a semester-long project (both written and oral) that focuses on the linkages among the disciplines of a scientific issue of their choice. Alternatively, the project can focus on developing and presenting an educational lesson plan. This would likely include presenting techniques on data collection, and how this issue can be presented to middle school students from a multidisciplinary viewpoint" (Rider University, 2006). All courses taken at the 200-level and 300-level are taken together with students majoring in one of the science or math majors. Those courses are selected from the areas of the life sciences, earth sciences, mathematics, and physical sciences.

BEGINNING THE BIBLIOGRAPHIC AND INFORMATION LITERACY SEQUENCE

The information literacy sequence begins with an assignment designed by the Biology and Teacher Preparation faculty members coteaching the introductory course. As the information literacy sequence is currently being introduced, an appropriate link between the introductory course and the capstone course is yet to be developed pending the establishment of the foundation of the sequence in the introductory course. Once the sequence is established in this foundational course, the connection between the introductory and capstone courses will be established. Next, the interdisciplinary faculty teaching the 200-level and 300-level courses will respond to information literacy objectives recommended by the science librarian for the intermediate-level courses. While we realize that this is not an optimal situation pedagogically since the students will need reinforcement of the skills at the 200 and 300 levels, we recognize the coordination that will need to take place among multiple departments and decided that it was important to be in a position to present the foundational experience. In the meantime, the science librarian will provide library instruction for as many of the 200- and 300-level courses as possible with the intent of both reinforcing and developing the science information literacy skills learned by ISM majors at the freshman level in addition to developing the science information literacy skills of the other science majors. The goal is to develop a model with the ISM majors that can then be replicated for other science majors.

INFORMATION LITERACY OBJECTIVES

The ISM information literacy objectives were adapted from the *Information Literacy Standards for Science and Engineering/Technology* (ALA/ACRL, 2006). It was considered necessary for these future teachers to be aware of a substantial amount of the hierarchy of knowledge production for the sciences since they will need to remain current in their knowledge of science developments and be able to encourage their own students to find information to answer their science questions.

The information literacy objectives that resulted following our discussion with the faculty members teaching the introductory course follow (see Figure 4.1). The objectives to be introduced at the beginning of the sequence have been identified by "freshman, 100-level."

ISM BIBLIOGRAPHIC AND INFORMATION LITERACY CURRICULUM AND ASSESSMENT OUTLINE

The following sequenced bibliographic and information literacy curriculum and recommended assessment method was developed for the ISM majors.

Introductory Level (*ISM-100, Introduction to the Integrated Sciences*)

Students in the introductory course (ISM-100) will be introduced to the ISM information literacy objectives and informed that they will be graded on their information

Objective A: Students will recognize the distinction between the scientific method and the hierarchy of knowledge production for the sciences. [Cognitive level: comprehension] [**FRESHMAN, 100-LEVEL**]

Objective B: Students will understand knowledge production for the sciences, including the ability to distinguish between and utilize primary, secondary, and tertiary types of research. This includes recognizing the value of archival information and its preservation requirements. [Cognitive levels: comprehension and application] [**FRESHMAN, 100-LEVEL**]

Objective C: Students will identify the position of the source in the cycle of scientific information production and recognize the credibility of the information based on that position. [Cognitive level: comprehension] [**FRESHMAN, 100-LEVEL**]

Objective D: Students will identify and make a distinction among a variety of types and formats of potential sources of information. These will include identifying and utilizing major science journals and recognizing popular vs. scholarly, current vs. historical, external vs. internal, primary vs. secondary vs. tertiary sources. [Cognitive levels: comprehension and application] [**FRESHMAN, 100-LEVEL**]

Objective E: Students will identify and investigate standard science sources (both print and electronic) used for specific purposes as well as by specific users (i.e., middle school students). These will include reference sources routinely used in the science professions (for example, encyclopedias, dictionaries, biographical sources, histories, handbooks, yearbooks, checklists, classification schemes, identification tools [field guides, manuals], book catalogs, statistical sources, legal sources [current rules and regulations], sources for standards, institutional policies, material/equipment specifications, product literature, book review sources, subject indexes and abstracts [both historical and current] of science journals and relevant scholarly and professional journals, relevant citation indexes, indexes to general periodicals [to determine general knowledge of the topic], indexes to relevant multidisciplinary sources, indexes to newspapers, relevant science Web sites including those of professional associations, and sources available to middle school students). [Cognitive levels: graduated skill development throughout sequence from knowledge to application]. [**FRESHMAN, 100-LEVEL**—knowledge level]

Objective F: Students will understand how government information is organized and identify the need to access information from municipal, state, federal, or international government sources and agencies, including the Environmental Protection Agency. [Cognitive level: application]

Objective G: Students will identify and utilize a variety of methods for keeping current in the field (e.g., following citation and cited references; using online table of contents scanning, review journals, and other rapid communication literature; managing files of citations; recognizing emerging forms and methods of scholarly publishing, e.g., blogs, freely available online research data). [Cognitive level: application]

Objective H: Students will compile a research log (and, later, a research plan) for their investigative method (e.g., literature search, laboratory experiment, simulation, fieldwork). The research log may include identifying appropriate keywords, synonyms, and related terms and identify a variety of types and formats of potential sources of information. [Cognitive level: application] [**FRESHMAN, 100-LEVEL**]

Objective I: Students will understand the range of resource availability and acquire needed material through means including interlibrary loan; nearby research libraries; requesting material from a group such as a government agency, public interest group, or organization. [Cognitive level: synthesis]

Objective J: Students will identify and document the potential usefulness of a source. [Cognitive levels: application and analysis]

Objective K: Students will be able to compare/contrast information from multiple sources in order to ensure the accuracy of the information used. This will include comparison of new knowledge with prior knowledge to determine the value added, contradictions, or other unique characteristics of the information. [Cognitive levels: analysis and synthesis]

Objective L: Students will apply the following evaluative skills to information: **distinguish among facts (reliability, validity, accuracy), authority, timeliness**, points of view, and opinion or bias; recognize and understand the impact on interpretation of the cultural, physical, or other context within which the information was created; analyze the structure and logic of supporting arguments or methods; understand and use statistical treatment of data as evaluative criteria; recognize prejudice, deception, or manipulation in information or its use. [Cognitive level: graduated skill development throughout sequence from analysis to synthesis to evaluation] [**FRESHMAN, 100-LEVEL** will emphasize those in **bold** above]

Objective M: Students will understand economic, legal, and social issues surrounding the use of information and access and use information ethically and legally, including recognizing copyright laws. They will appropriately acknowledge their sources, including appropriately acknowledging quotations, accurately quoting, paraphrasing, and avoiding plagiarism. [Cognitive level: application] [**FRESHMAN, 100-LEVEL**]

Objective N: Students will understand knowledge production (both print and electronic) for science curricular resources to support students in middle school grades. [Cognitive level: comprehension]

Objective O: In preparation for the middle school classroom experience and for selecting appropriate curricular resources (e.g., textbook selection), students will identify, locate, and utilize parts of a book such as title, author(s), illustrator(s), spine and label, title page, verso page, publisher and place of publication, copyright date, preface/forward/introduction, table of contents, text, illustrations and their captions, footnotes, index, glossary, appendix, bibliography. [Cognitive level: comprehension]

Objective P: Students will be able to effectively understand, analyze, evaluate, synthesize, compare/contrast, and apply information from individual and multiple sources in order to ensure the accuracy of information used. [Cognitive levels: analysis and synthesis]

Figure 4.1 Information Literacy Objectives for the Integrated Sciences and Math Major.

literacy proficiency in the capstone course (where they will be expected to produce (for a grade) a research plan for a literature search (see Objective H, ahead) for projects in the capstone course.

Since the students in ISM-100 will include both first-semester freshmen and upper-level transfer students from another major, some will not have taken the required Research Writing course within which there is an information literacy component (while some may be taking Research Writing simultaneously with ISM-100). While the skills learned in the Research Writing course are actively reinforced and intended to transfer to and be complementary with skills learned in other courses, it is the intent that the science information literacy instruction will be discipline-specific and not repetitive.

A brief introduction to the science librarian and to the library's science resources will occur near the beginning of the semester. Course-embedded information literacy skills will then be learned independently throughout the semester to coordinate with the inquiry approach taken by the professors. There will be several brief assignments and a larger quantitative data-collection assignment requiring background information to support the hypothesis and experiment design. The shorter assignments will occur periodically as students develop their own questions in response to class discussion, readings or outside readings of current science topics in the news. They will be prompted by their professors to consider, "How would I answer this question?" and "Where would I look for this information?"

They will need to research the answers to their questions and will be expected to meet with the science librarian, or with a designated librarian who has been cross-trained by the science librarian for the ISM sequence. Each student will maintain a research log made available via the library's Web page. The intent of the log is to keep track of their sources used for each assignment, to note the type of source (i.e., popular science journal, professional science journal, etc.), and whether or not they might expect to find such a source in their middle school. In this way, the student will be learning about the science sources as they are discovered in the process of answering their question(s). This process is intended to complement the inquiry approach taken in the course. There is no way to predict ahead of time which sources will be used and it is expected that each student will use different sources. Reference to the Science Subject Guides available on the library's Web page will be made during the research process to prompt the student with suggestions. Reinforcement of the type(s) of literature used to answer the question(s) is intended to acquaint the student with the purpose of the literature and its position within the hierarchy of knowledge production for the sciences. This bibliographic and information literacy approach will occur for both the short assignments and for the larger assignment. The final electronic copy of the research log will remain available for each student to retain and for use as a reference in upcoming classes.

We recognize the difficulty of replicating this individualized process in a larger institution and emphasize the cross-training component of this process. The cross-training could take place with ISM seniors to reinforce their learning of information literacy skills as they teach freshmen and could take place with science honors students as well as graduate students.

Assessment method: Students will review their research logs (see Figure 4.2) and the introductory-level ISM Information Literacy Learning Objectives with the science librarian and indicate the skills mastered and their individual needs for improvement. The science librarian and the course professors will review the research paths and the resulting projects to identify future improvements needed to support the research process.

SOURCE CONSULTED (e.g., *McGraw-Hill Encyclopedia of Science and Technology; JAMA; Popular Science*)	HOW I DISCOVERED THIS SOURCE	WHAT TYPE OF SOURCE IS IT? (e.g., a popular science magazine? a professional science journal?)	IS THIS SOURCE AVAILABLE IN A MIDDLE SCHOOL MEDIA CENTER?	WOULD THIS SOURCE BE USEFUL FOR MY FUTURE STUDENTS AT THE MIDDLE SCHOOL LEVEL?	CHECK (√) IF THE SOURCE WAS USED AGAIN FOR ANOTHER QUESTION (You may have multiple checks)
RESEARCH QUESTION					
RESEARCH QUESTION					

Figure 4.2 Student Research Log.

Intermediate Level *(200-level and 300-level courses)*

Course-embedded information literacy skills will be taught wherever possible to reinforce the skills learned in the introductory levels and to introduce higher-level skills. Reinforcement of cross-learning of information literacy skills (i.e., Chemistry and Physics) will also occur.

Assessment method: Students will be reintroduced to the ISM information literacy objectives and will continue to add sources to their research logs initiated in the freshman year. During their student teaching observations, they will note sources used with students in the middle school classrooms and media centers. Students will also meet with the science librarian at least once in a semester during their sophomore and junior years. To enable these contacts, the Science Librarian has arranged for an office in Science Hall to be used periodically throughout the semester to provide science reference to faculty and students. Professors teaching courses in the ISM major will determine the effectiveness of the students' research process based upon the resulting products (e.g., papers, presentations). Recommendations from the professors for reinforcement of specific information literacy skills will be provided to the librarians who will be reinforcing the skills in the capstone course.

Advanced Level *(Capstone course: ISM-410, Seminar in the Integrated Sciences)*

Reinforcement of earlier skills will be done as recommended by professors. Emphasis will be on Objectives K & L related to the critical analysis of the scientific literature.

"No matter how information is presented, whether it's as a research article or as one in a popular newsstand magazine, it is important to read that information critically in order to evaluate it. The following ideas are *suggestions* to think about while reading. This is not an all-inclusive list nor will every idea be applicable to every article you read. But if you keep these ideas in mind as you read, they should be able to help you analyze and assess the information being presented.

Nature of the Information and Documentation

1. What is the nature of the information presented?
   Original data?
   Summaries of original data?
   Anecdotal information?
   Background information?
   Interpretation of original data and explanation of significance?
2. What is the nature of the documentation?
   Is supporting evidence given?
   Are sources for that evidence clearly documented?
   Are sources for that evidence appropriate?
   What are the credentials of the sources?
   Are the sources current?

Purpose and Intended Audience

3. What is (are) the purposes of the article?
   To describe (What happened)?
   To explain (Why did it happen?)
   To interpret (What does it mean?)
   To entertain?
4. Who is the intended audience?
   General reader?
   Professionals in the same discipline?
   Professionals in other disciplines?

Credentials

5. What are the credentials of the author?
   Is there an identified author(s)?
   Did the author do the research?
   Is the author someone who's working in the field?
   What is the author's point of view?
   Does the author have a bias?
6. What are the credentials of the journal/magazine?
   Is it peer-reviewed?
   What is the reputation of the journal?
   Is it published by a professional association and if so, what do you know about the reputation of this association?
   Is it published for profit?
   What role does the profit motive play in the selection of articles for this journal/magazine?
7. Is a funding source or site for the research described identified?
   Does that funding source imply a bias?

Figure 4.3 Don't Believe Everything you Read: Ideas for Reading Critically about Science.
Source: Loomis, Abbie, and Patricia Herrling. "Don't Believe Everything You Read: Ideas for Reading Critically about Science." Handout developed by the Library & Information Literacy Instruction Program, University of Wisconsin-Madison. Included in Loomis, Abbie, and Patricia Herrling, "Course-Integrated Honors Instruction: Pros and Cons." In *What is Good Instruction Now? Library Instruction for the 90 s.* Papers and session materials presented at the 20th National LOEX Library Instruction Conference held at Eastern Michigan University, May 8–9, 1992. Ann Arbor, MI: Pierian Press, 1993, 93–102. Reprinted with permission.

Presentation and Style

8. How is the information presented?
   Is the research placed in a context (i.e., do you know why it was done?)
   Is the methodology stated with enough detail to be replicated?
   Is the significance of the results clear?
9. What is the style of the article?
   Is it well-written?
   What is the nature of the language used?
   Easy to understand for general reader?
   Technical?
   Objective?
   Emotionally charged?
   What is the level of detail in the article?
   Are the language and level of detail used appropriate for the intended audience and the purpose?
10. What kinds of illustrations are included (e.g., graphs, photos, drawings, etc.)?
    Are the illustrations appropriate to the content and style of the article?
    What is the purpose of the illustrations?
    Do the illustrations have captions and are these clear and appropriate?
    Are there hidden messages to the illustrations?"

Figure 4.3 (continued)

For this purpose, the librarians agreed to develop a guide to critical analysis of scientific literature (made available at the libraries' Web site) to provide students with support in this process in the upper-level courses. A recommended example (see Figure 4.3) of such a critical analysis is provided by Loomis and Herrling (1993).

Assessment method: Students will consult the research log begun during and updated since the freshman year for its use in preparing a research plan for a literature search for their project(s) in the seminar (see Objective H). They will continue to update the log as they discover sources used in their middle school student teaching experiences. Librarian(s) will consult with and respond to each student with additional source recommendations. Students will demonstrate their ability to evaluate at least five sources used for their final works cited list by referring to a guide to critical analysis of scientific literature made available at the libraries' Web site. The research log and a completed research plan for a literature search will be submitted at the end of the capstone course together with the source evaluations. Students will be graded according to a rubric developed to coordinate with the ISM information literacy objectives introduced to students in the introductory level and reintroduced (as appropriate) to students in the intermediate levels. The levels of proficiency reached will be determined programmatically by compiling a summary of all students' rubric data. Librarians and professors will review the results to determine the students' levels of proficiency at the cognitive stages of analysis, synthesis, and evaluation. Recommendations for improvements to the information literacy sequence will be made.

REFERENCES

American Library Association (ALA), Association of College and Research Libraries (ACRL), STS Task Force on Information Literacy for Science and Technology (2006). *Information Literacy Standards for Science and Engineering/Technology*. http://www.ala.org/ala/acrl/acrlstandards/infolitscitech.cfm (accessed March 13, 2008).

Loomis, Abbie, and Patricia Herrling. "Don't Believe Everything you Read: Ideas for Reading Critically about Science." Handout developed by the Library & Information Literacy Instruction Program, University of Wisconsin-Madison. Included in Loomis, Abbie, and Patricia Herrling, "Course-integrated Honors Instruction: Pros and Cons." In *What is Good Instruction Now? Library Instruction for the 90s*. Papers and session materials presented at the 20th National LOEX Library Instruction Conference held at Eastern Michigan University, May 8–9, 1992, ed. Linda Shirato, 93–102. Ann Arbor, MI: Pierian Press, 1993.

Rider University. *Undergraduate Catalog 06/07*. Lawrenceville, NJ: Rider University, 2006.

ADDITIONAL READINGS

Adalian, Paul T., Jr. "Use of Media News in Bibliographic Instruction: An Application in a Biological Literature Course." In *What is Good Instruction Now? Library Instruction for the 90s*, ed. Linda Shirato, 31–36. Ann Arbor, MI: Pierian Press, 1993.

Bowden, Teresa S., and Angela DiBenedetto. "Information Literacy in a Biology Laboratory Session: An Example of Librarian-Faculty Collaboration." *Research Strategies* 18 (2001): 143–149.

Brown, Cecelia, and Lee R. Krumholz. "Integrating Information Literacy into the Science Curriculum." *College & Research Libraries* 63(2) (2002): 111–123.

Burry-Stock, Judith A. and Rebecca L. Oxford. "Expert Science Teaching Educational Evaluation Model (ESTEEM): Measuring Excellence in Science Teaching for Professional Development." *Journal of Personnel Evaluation in Education* 8 (1994): 267–297.

Church, Gary Mason, and Brian B. Carpenter. "The Life in Inventions: Patents as Sources of Biological Information." *Issues in Science and Technology Librarianship* (Fall 2000). http://www.istl.org/00-fall/article5.html (accessed March 13, 2006).

Kirk, Thomas. "Shaping a Bibliographic Instruction Program for Undergraduate Science Students: Applications of a Model of the Structure of Scientific Literature." In *Back to the Books: Bibliographic Instruction and the Theory of Information Sources*, ed. Ross Atkinson, 57–70. Chicago: Association of College and Research Libraries, American Library Association, 1983.

Laherty, J. "Promoting Information Literacy for Science Education Programs: Correlating the National Science Education Standards with the Association of College and Research Libraries Information Competency Standards for Higher Education." *Issues in Science and Technology Librarianship* 28 (2000). http://www.istl.org/00-fall/article3.html (accessed August 10, 2006).

Martin, Rebecca R. "Library Instruction and the Scientific Method: A Role for Librarians in an Introductory Biology Course." *Research Strategies* 4(3) (1986): 108–115.

Mohler, Beth. A. "Citation Analysis as an Assessment Tool." *Science & Technology Libraries* 25(4) (2005): 57–64.

Newby, Jill. "Evolution of a Library Research Methods Course for Biology Students." *Research Strategies* 17 (2000): 57–62.

Orians, Colin, and Laurie Sabol. "Using the Web to Teach Library Research Skills in Introductory Biology: A Collaboration between Faculty and Librarians." *Issues in Science and Technology Librarianship* (Summer 1999). http://www.istl.org/99-summer/article2.html (accessed March 13, 2006).

Penhale, Sara J., Jerome H. Woolpy, and William H. Buskirk. "Learning to be a Responsible Patient." *Research Strategies* 9 (Winter 1991): 51–55.

Sinn, Robin N. "A Comparison of Library Instruction Content by Biology Faculty and Librarians." *Research Strategies* 17 (2000): 23–34.

5

Recommended Sequence for Bibliographic and Information Literacy: Teacher Preparation

BACKGROUND: LIBRARIANS AS POLITICAL PLAYERS

Several years ago, I spoke with an administrator of the teacher preparation program and mentioned the information literacy requirements that were recommended for our state's K-12 curriculum. I noted the importance of teaching these skills to our future teachers so that they, in turn, will be prepared to teach the skills to their future students. I was quickly dismissed by a comment indicating that the students in the teacher preparation program already had so many requirements imposed upon them by outside accreditors that she saw no reason to add to those requirements.

In the meantime, I shared some literature gathered at a conference and the state's recommended K-12 information literacy curriculum with one of the professors in the program. His daughter had recently completed an internship in our library, had earned her master's degree in library and information science and was now an elementary school librarian. His son was a high school English teacher who had great appreciation for his school's librarian. Soon afterward, one of our librarians, who is particularly successful as a liaison, made a concerted effort to introduce library instruction into more courses in the teacher preparation program, including those of the professor whom I had also contacted.

The university began a strategic planning process in 2004, and three librarians became involved on three separate committees. During this process, we recognized the need to meet with the academic strategic planning committee to ensure that the instructional role of the libraries was clearly identified in their report. The final strategic plan for our university defines information literacy (see Introduction) and includes the recommendation for further integrating information literacy into the curriculum.

The strategic plan also identified the need to identify common learning competencies, or general education requirements, and a task force was created for this purpose that included a librarian. The librarian who has led the library's assessment effort was invited to discuss information literacy with the task force and the report of the task force includes information literacy as one of the common learning competencies. Upon approval of the task force's recommendation, each department will be required to include each of the common learning competencies in its goals and then will be required to assess them.

With this sequence of events in mind, I spoke again with the administrator of the teacher preparation program about a proposal that I was developing for an information literacy sequence for majors in teacher preparation. This time, she was very enthusiastic and encouraged me to talk with the chairperson of the department as soon as possible. And, this time, she agreed that our efforts to ensure that majors in the teacher preparation program are information literate offered an opportunity to be "teaching twice" since their skills could be passed along to a whole new generation that will be better prepared for their college experience. Needless to say, though, I had also prepared well to justify the proposal by recognizing that the teacher preparation program must address state, national, and organizational standards in order to fulfill their reaccreditation requirements. And, as an additional justification, the following quote from the Center for an Urban Future was included in the proposal.

According to the Center for an Urban Future's 2001 report, *Building a Highway to Higher Ed: How Collaborative Efforts are Changing Education in America*, "three-quarters of all high school graduates are now entering a four-year or community college within two years of graduation—and hundreds of thousands are failing or bailing out because they are utterly unprepared when they arrive. Nationwide, some 30 percent of college students arrive at college campuses in need of remedial classes. And despite the impressive number of students throughout the country who are giving it the old college try, over 50 percent of them fail to earn a degree; one-third of these students never even see their sophomore year, according to the Education Trust" (Kleiman, 2001). Carr and Rockman (2003, 52) elaborate that "in today's information-rich world, a contributing factor to that high rate of failure is the inability of students in higher education to find and use information effectively. The need to increase retention and completion rates for students in higher education is a compelling reason for academic librarians to collaborate with their K-12 colleagues in developing information-literacy activities across K-20 education."

This experience is probably a familiar one for librarians, who recognize the benefits of bibliographic and information literacy skills for our students, but who have a difficult time conveying the importance to faculty in some disciplines. In the in-between years, we were active politically to influence the university community from the strategic planning level to college administrators to disciplinary faculty. Our patience and persistence have paid off.

BIBLIOGRAPHIC AND INFORMATION LITERACY PROPOSAL FOR TEACHER PREPARATION

The recommendation for teacher preparation has three considerations: the professional development of the teacher, developing the teacher's ability to identify resources for students in his/her classroom, and developing the teacher's ability to instruct students in his/her classroom about skills for seeking information that extends the learning experience beyond the classroom. This process promotes continuing learning experiences for both the teacher and the students in his/her classroom. With this intent, there will be a coordinated effort between the librarians and the staff of the education resource center to promote resource use by students. (The education resource center provides curricular support for the teacher preparation program. Many libraries have a similar K-12 education collection incorporated into the university library's collection.) It is also recommended that students in the teacher preparation program will develop a connection with the librarian in the school library media center of their field experience placement.

The process of developing the proposal began with a curriculum map for the major (see Chapter 1), an identification of the department's assessment goals and a review of course syllabi. The syllabi referenced state, national, and organizational education standards which were also reviewed. Next, state and national information literacy standards developed for the K-12 curriculum were identified and reviewed. The conclusion of this process was to develop information literacy objectives for the teacher preparation program.

Step 1: Education and Organizational Standards

Check the state and national standards to which your teacher preparation program refers. Several education standards and references to related materials were identified in our teacher preparation syllabi and reviewed. They included the *Interstate New Teacher Assessment and Support Consortium (INTASC) Standards* developed by the Council of Chief State School Officers (CCSSO) and member states, the New Jersey Department of Education *Core Curriculum Content Standards and Frameworks*, New Jersey Special Education Code, New Jersey State Board of Education *English Language Proficiency Standards*, Council for Exceptional Children Standards, Standards of the National Council for the Social Studies (NCSS), and the Standards of the National Council of Teachers of English (NCTE).

Often these standards include information literacy standards, as, for example: "students read a wide range of print and non-print texts to build an understanding of texts, of themselves, and of the cultures of the United States and the world; to acquire new information; to respond to the needs and demands of society and the workplace; and for personal fulfillment. Among these texts are fiction and nonfiction, classic and contemporary works . . . Students apply a wide range of strategies to comprehend, interpret, evaluate, and appreciate texts . . . Students conduct research on issues and interests by generating ideas and questions, and by posing problems . . . Students use a variety of technological and informational resources (e.g., libraries, databases, computer networks, video) to gather and synthesize information and to create and communicate knowledge" (National Council of Teachers of English and the International Reading Association (NCTE/IRA) *Standards for the English Language Arts*).

Step 2: Information Literacy Standards for the K-12 Curriculum

Check to see if there is a K-12 or P-20 information literacy plan in your state or in the school districts in which the students in the teacher preparation program complete their student teaching requirements. There are several concerted efforts to refer to if you are interested in initiating a movement in your region (Kleiman, 2001; Carr and Rockman, 2003). Several K-12 information literacy standards were identified and reviewed.

> **Understands Content**: Principle #1: "The teacher understands the central concepts, **tools of inquiry**, and structures of the discipline(s) he or she teaches and **can create learning experiences that make these aspects of subject matter meaningful for students**."
>
> **Understands Development**: Principle #2: "The teacher understands how children learn and develop, and **can provide learning opportunities that support their intellectual, social, and personal development**."
>
> Understands Difference: Principle #3: "The teacher understands how students differ in their approaches to learning and creates instructional opportunities that are adapted to diverse learners."
>
> **Designs Instructional Strategies**: Principle #4: "The teacher **understands and uses a variety of instructional strategies** to encourage students' development of critical thinking, problem solving, and performance skills."
>
> Manages and Motivates: Principle #5: "The teacher uses an understanding of individual and group motivation and behavior to create a learning environment that encourages positive social interaction, active engagement in learning and self-motivation."
>
> **Communicates**: Principle # 6: "The teacher uses knowledge of effective verbal, nonverbal, and **media communication techniques to foster active inquiry**, collaboration, and supportive interaction in the classroom."
>
> Plans and Integrates: Principle #7: "The teacher plans instruction based upon knowledge of subject matter, students, the community, and curriculum goals."
>
> Evaluates: Principle #8: "The teacher understands and uses formal and informal assessment strategies to evaluate and ensure the continuous intellectual, social, and physical development of the learner."
>
> **Reflects on Practice**: Principle #9: "The teacher is a reflective practitioner who continually evaluates the effects of his/her choices and actions on others (students, parents, and other professionals in the learning community) and who **actively seeks out opportunities to grow professionally**."
>
> **Participates in the Professional Community**: Principle #10: "The teacher **fosters relationships with school colleagues**, parents, **and agencies in the larger community to support students' learning** and well-being." [consider school library media specialists and public librarians.]

Figure 5.1 Interstate New Teacher Assessment and Support Consortium (INTASC) Standards (bold **indicates areas addressed by the information literacy sequence**).
Source: Council of Chief State School Officers. "Model Standards for Beginning Teacher Licensing, Assessment, and Development: A Resource for State Dialogue." (1992). Washington, DC: Council of Chief State School Officers. http://www.ccsso.org/content/pdfs/corestrd.pdf. Reprinted with permission.

They included the *Blueprint for Collaboration* (AASL/ACRL, 2000), *School Library Media Curriculum Template* (Educational Media Association of New Jersey [EMAnj], 2000), *Information Power* (AASL/AECT, 1998), and *Information Problem-Solving: The Big 6 Skills Approach to Library and Information Skills* (Eisenberg and Berkowitz, 1990).

Step 3: The Library's Support for the Teacher Preparation Assessment Goals

The assessment goals of the Teacher Preparation Department are linked to the INTASC Standards. These standards were developed by the CCSSO and member states. Copies may be downloaded from the Council's Web site at http://www.ccsso.org. CCSSO is a nonpartisan, nationwide, nonprofit organization of public officials who head departments of elementary and secondary education in the states, the District of Columbia, the Department of Defense Education Activity, and five U. S. extra-state jurisdictions. CCSSO provides leadership, advocacy, and technical assistance on major educational issues. The Council seeks member consensus on major educational issues and expresses their views to civic and professional organizations, federal agencies, Congress, and the public. After reviewing the INTASC standards, it was decided that the library will concentrate on supporting the INTASC principles (see Figure 5.1) identified in **bold**.

Step 4: Relating the Information Literacy Standards to the Education Standards

Since there is the opportunity to "teach twice," the next step is to consider the standards for the students in the P-12 classroom together with the standards for the undergraduate students in the teacher preparation program. Carr and Rockman (2003) compared the information literacy standards (see Figure 5.2) (a.k.a. "information power" standards) developed by the American Association of School Librarians (AASL) and the Association for Educational Communications and Technology (AECT) to the standards developed by the Association of College and Research Libraries (ACRL). While reviewing this comparison, we continued to identify the INTASC Principle(s) that each standard related to.

Step 5: Developing Bibliographic and Information Literacy Objectives for the Teacher Preparation Program

Now it was time to use all of the referenced material to develop the information literacy objectives for majors in our teacher preparation program. Each of the following objectives (see Figure 5.3) identifies the INTASC Principle that is being supported by the objective and the relationship to either the relevant ACRL or AASL/AECT Standard. Objectives that are to be introduced in the introductory level of the program are identified.

Step 6: Developing the Skill Sequence

Now it was time to combine the curriculum map with the assignments identified in the syllabi in order to identify the information literacy skills that were currently being taught in the course (see column in Figure 5.4 titled: "Course Description and Information Literacy Skills Currently Identified in Syllabi"). For each course, we included the course description, a description of the assignment (the descriptions have been abbreviated here, but for our actual curriculum maps we have included detailed assignment information), the information literacy objectives currently included in the syllabi, and the current cognitive level of information literacy skill required in the course.

We then identified the objectives that should most logically be taught within each course in order to develop an appropriate sequence of skill development (see column titled: "Information Literacy Skills [and Cognitive Level] Required for this Course"). With the comparison between the objectives currently required and those recommended, we looked more closely at the actual skills being taught. We realized that even though an information literacy objective was identified in the syllabi, there may have been only one aspect of the objective that was actually taught. For example, while Objective A requires an understanding and application of knowledge production for the education profession, students may, in fact, only be introduced to an indexed education database. We also noted that, depending upon the particular assignments in the course, the students' opportunity to practice a variety of skills was inconsistent. We were also aware from our reference

STANDARDS: AASL vs. ACRL	
Information Power Standards **(AASL/AECT)** (http://www.ala.org/acrl/ilcomstan.html) *(For students in the P-12 classroom)*	**Information Literacy Competency** **Standards for Higher Education** **(ACRL)** (http://www.ala.org/acrl/blueprint.html) *(For students in the teacher preparation program)*

INFORMATION LITERACY:
STANDARD 1: The student who is information literate accesses information efficiently and effectively. (*Relates to INTASC Principle #1,2,4*)
STANDARD 2: The student who is information literate evaluates information critically and competently. (*Relates to INTASC Principle #2*)
STANDARD 3: The student who is information literate uses information accurately and creatively. (*Relates to INTASC Principle #1,2,4*)

Standard 1: The information-literate student determines the nature and extent of the information needed. (*Relates to INTASC Principle #1,2,4,5,6,9,10*)

INDEPENDENT LEARNING:
STANDARD 4: The student who is an independent learner is information literate and pursues information related to personal interests. (*Relates to INTASC Principle #1,2*)
STANDARD 5: The student who is an independent learner is information literate and appreciates literature and other creative expressions of information. (*Relates to INTASC Principle #1,2*)
STANDARD 6: The student who is an independent learner is information literate and strives for excellence in information seeking and knowledge generation. (*Relates to INTASC Principle #1,2,3*)

Standard 2: The information-literate student accesses needed information effectively and efficiently. (*Relates to INTASC Principle #1,2,4,6,9*)
Standard 3: The information-literate student evaluates information and its sources critically and incorporates selected information into his or her knowledge base and value system. (*Relates to INTASC Principle #1,4,9*)

SOCIAL RESPONSIBILITY:
STANDARD 7: The student who contributes positively to the learning community and to society is information literate and recognizes the importance of information to a democratic society. (*Relates to INTASC Principle #2*)
STANDARD 8: The student who contributes positively to the learning community and to society is information literate and practices ethical behavior in regard to information and information technology. (*Relates to INTASC Principle #2*)
STANDARD 9: The student who contributes positively to the learning community and to society is information literate and participates effectively in groups to pursue and generate information. (*Relates to INTASC Principle #2*)

Standard 4: The information-literate student, individually or as a member of a group, uses information effectively to accomplish a specific purpose. (*Relates to INTASC Principle #1,2,4,9,10*)

Standard 5: The information-literate student understands many of the economic, legal, and social issues surrounding the use of information and accesses and uses information ethically and legally. (*Relates to INTASC Principle #2*)

Figure 5.2 Information Literacy Standards (AASL/AECT and ACRL) (*These standards are incorporated into the information literacy objectives recommended ahead*).
Source: Adapted from "Standards: AASL vs ACRL." [figure] In Carr, Jo Ann, & Rockman, Ilene F. (2003). Information-literacy collaboration: A shared responsibility. *American Libraries* 34(8), 52–54. Reprinted with permission.

Objective A: Students in the teacher preparation program will understand knowledge production for the professional development of the teacher preparation profession, including the ability to identify primary, secondary, and tertiary literature and appropriately identify and effectively use (both print and electronic) bibliographies, dictionaries, encyclopedias, directories, almanacs, guides, handbooks, yearbooks, statistical sources, biographies, relevant government documents, book catalogs, indexes and abstracts to education literature (including education journals and ERIC documents), indexes and abstracts to relevant interdisciplinary literature (e.g., psychology, major national newspapers), relevant Web sites (including relevant teacher associations and relevant state and national standards). [Cognitive level: application; introduced at the **introductory level**; supports INTASC Principle #1, 9; relates to ACRL Standard #1, 2, 3]

Objective B: Students will understand knowledge production for (both print and electronic) curricular resources to support students in grades P-12. [Cognitive level: comprehension; introduced at the **junior level**; supports INTASC Principle #1, 2; relates to ACRL Standard #1]

Objective C: Students will understand that libraries serve different purposes, are arranged differently, and that all provide a diverse collection of information presenting many viewpoints. Students will utilize at least the school library media center, the education resource center, the university libraries, and public libraries to support their research and curricular enhancement needs. [Cognitive level: application; introduced at the **junior level**; supports INTASC Principle #1, 4, 9, 10; relates to ACRL Standard #1, 2, 3]

Objective D: Students will utilize and collaborate with the school library media specialist as a teacher and resource person (storyteller, literature consultant, reference consultant, research consultant, selector/purchaser, technology consultant). [Cognitive level: application; introduced at the **junior level**; supports INTASC Principle #1, 4, 9, 10; relates to ACRL Standard #1, 2, 4]

Objective E: Students will identify primary, secondary, and tertiary literature and effectively use appropriate resources (both print and electronic) to support and enhance the classroom curricular experience, resource-based learning and recreational reading of students in grades P-12. Resources will be obtained from libraries, bookstores, free Web sites, and/or teacher supply stores. Resources will include textbook publishers' catalogs, nonfiction literature for P-12, fiction literature for P-12 (including easy/picture books), biography, story collections, magazines (entertainment, news, special interests), newspapers, vertical files, academic databases, reference sources (including encyclopedias, guides, dictionaries, almanacs, biographical sources, handbooks, yearbooks, statistical sources, atlases), and manipulatives. [Cognitive level: application; introduced at the **junior level**; supports INTASC Principle #1, 2, 4, 11; relates to AASL/AECT Standard #1, 4, 5, 6; relates to ACRL Standard #1, 2, 3, 4]

Objective F: In preparation for the classroom experience and for selecting appropriate curricular resources (e.g., textbook selection), students will identify, locate, and utilize parts of a book, i.e., title, author(s), illustrator(s), spine and label, title page, verso page, publisher and place of publication, copyright date, preface/forward/introduction, table of contents, text, illustrations and their captions, footnotes, index, glossary, appendix, bibliography. [Cognitive level: comprehension; introduced at the **junior level**; supports INTASC Principle #1; relates to ACRL Standard #3]

Objective G: Students will judge the value of a resource by noting its reliability, validity, accuracy, authority, timeliness, point of view or bias. [Graduated skill development throughout sequence from cognitive levels of knowledge to evaluation; introduced at the **introductory level**; supports INTASC Principle #2, 4, 11; relates to AASL/AECT Standard #2, 3, 6, 7, 8; relates to ACRL Standard #5]

Objective H: Students will be able to effectively understand, analyze, evaluate, synthesize, compare/contrast, and apply information from individual and multiple sources in order to ensure the accuracy of information used. [Graduated skill development from cognitive levels of analysis to synthesis to evaluation; introduced at the **junior level**; supports INTASC Principle #2, 11; relates to AASL/AECT Standard #2, 3, 6, 7, 8, 9; relates to ACRL Standard #3, 5]

Objective I: Students will understand economic, legal, and social issues surrounding the use of information and access and use information ethically and legally, including recognizing copyright laws. Students will appropriately acknowledge their sources according to the style of the American Psychological Association (APA), including appropriately acknowledging quotations, accurately quoting, paraphrasing, and avoiding plagiarism. [Cognitive level: application; introduced at the **introductory level**; supports INTASC Principle #1; relates to AASL/AECT Standards #6, 7, 8, 9; relates to ACRL Standard #5]

Figure 5.3 Information Literacy Objectives for Teacher Preparation.

COURSE	LIBRARY INSTRUCTION (∗) or Opportunity	COURSE DESCRIPTION & INFORMATION LITERACY SKILLS <u>CURRENTLY</u> <u>IDENTIFIED</u> IN SYLLABI (*Source for descriptions*: Rider University. **Undergraduate Catalog 06/07**. Lawrenceville, New Jersey: Rider University, 2006.)	INFORMATION LITERACY SKILL(S) (AND COGNITIVE LEVEL) REQUIRED FOR THIS COURSE	SPECIFIC SKILLS <u>CURRENTLY</u> TAUGHT & TEACHING IMPROVEMENTS NEEDED
EDU-010- Cohort Seminar (*Sophomore level*)	Opportunity	*Course description*: *"Designed for students new to education, this seminar is a small-group experience that serves as an orientation to the program. Concerns about preparing to be a professional as well as academic and personal development are considered in one-hour weekly sessions. The one supplemental education unit does not count toward graduation; grading is on a pass/fail basis."* *Assignment*: *To be developed* **Information Literacy Objectives** *(currently): NA* **Cognitive level required** *(currently): NA*	***Information Literacy Objectives*** *(required)*: A, G (Knowledge level), I ***Cognitive level required***: Application	***Information Literacy skills currently taught***: None ***Teaching Improvements needed***: NA (opportunity)
EDU-100- Contexts of Schooling (*Sophomore level*)	∗	*Course description*: *"Students in this field-based course will begin to examine aims, practices, and contemporary issues of schooling in their historical, sociological, philosophical, and futuristic contexts and from the perspectives of various multicultural constituencies—students, parents, local community, wider economic community, government, and the profession. In doing so, they will begin to develop professional skills of observation, reflection, analysis, and argument."* *Assignment*: Research papers; citing scholarly sources. **Information Literacy Objectives** *(currently)*: A, I **Cognitive level required** *(currently)*: Application	***Information Literacy Objectives*** *(required)*: A, G (Knowledge- Application level), I ***Cognitive level required***: Application	***Information Literacy skills currently taught***: Obj A: Education indexed databases (professional literature including education journals and ERIC documents) Obj I: Citations ***Reinforcement of skills needed***: A, G, I ***Teaching Improvements needed***: Obj A (expand): Utilize: scholarly education encyclopedias/yearbooks, book catalogs Introduce relevant interdisciplinary literature: sociology sources, government information, national newspapers Obj G: Emphasize the authority, point of view/bias of a source
EDU-200- Developmental Educational Psychology (*Sophomore level*)	∗	*Course description*: *"This field-based course focuses on (a) the cognitive, personality, social, creative, and moral development of children; (b) influential theories, concepts, and research findings of educational psychology; and (c) the translation of psychological theory into classroom practices."* *Assignment*: Research related to educational psychology.	***Information Literacy Objectives*** *(required)*: A, G (Knowledge- Application level), I ***Cognitive level required***: Application	***Information Literacy skills currently taught***: Obj A: Education indexed databases (professional literature including education journals and ERIC documents); relevant interdisciplinary literature (Psychology indexed databases) ***Reinforcement of skills needed***: A, G, I

Figure 5.4 Bibliographic and Information Literacy Sequence for Teacher Preparation.

	Information Literacy Objectives (currently): A, I *Cognitive level required (currently):* Application		*Teaching Improvements needed:* Obj A (expand): Utilize: book catalogs Obj G: Emphasize the authority, point of view/bias of a source
ELD-300-Emergent Literacy P-3 (*Junior level*)	*	*Course description:* "This course is needed to meet the requirements for the specialized endorsement in Early Childhood. The course establishes a solid foundation of knowledge about literacy in the early years and dispels myths regarding readiness to read and write. In addition, the course contains the foundational aspects of literacy, including the relationship between oral language and literacy, the linguistic foundation of literacy, and the social contexts of literacy learning." *Assignment:* Research related to teaching observation; lesson plans, annotated bibliography; case study. *Information Literacy Objectives (currently):* A, B, C, D, E, I *Cognitive level required (currently):* Comprehension Application	*Information Literacy Objectives (required):* A, B, C, D, E, F, G (Analysis-Synthesis level), H (Analysis-Synthesis level), I *Cognitive level required:* Knowledge Comprehension Application Analysis Synthesis	*Information Literacy skills currently taught:* Obj A: Education indexed databases (professional literature including education journals and ERIC documents); relevant interdisciplinary literature (Psychology indexed databases) *Reinforcement of skills needed:* A, G, I *Teaching Improvements needed:* Obj A: (expand): Utilize: book catalogs Obj B: Emphasize knowledge production of curricular resources Obj C: Introduce students to various library collections available Obj D: Introduce students to the school library media specialist Obj E: Emphasize sources for classroom curricular resource support Obj F: Preparation for curricular selection Obj G: Emphasize reliability, validity, accuracy authority, timeliness, point of view/bias of information Obj H: Emphasize the need to compare/contrast information in different sources
ELD-300-Fostering Language & Literacy Development (*Junior level*)	*	*Course description:* "Explores current understanding of the fields of reading/language arts from the perspectives of theory and practice. Students write lesson plans, critique methods of instruction and assessment and develop a portfolio of an individual student from their field site." *Assignment:* Select teaching materials (including K-5 resources), design lesson plan supported by article in peer-reviewed journal, develop curriculum unit supported by articles in peer-reviewed journals, identify assessment techniques. *Information Literacy Objectives (currently):* A, B, C, D, E, G, H, I	*Information Literacy Objectives (required):* A, B, C, D, E, F, G (Analysis-Synthesis level), H (Analysis-Synthesis level), I *Cognitive level required:* Knowledge Comprehension Application Analysis Synthesis	*Information Literacy skills currently taught:* Thorough information literacy skill integration in this course. *Reinforcement of skills needed:* Obj A, G, I *Teaching Improvements needed:* Obj A: (expand): Utilize: book catalogs Obj B: Emphasize knowledge production of curricular resources Obj C: Emphasize various library collections available Obj D: Emphasize use of the school library media specialist Obj E: Emphasize sources for classroom curricular resource support

Figure 5.4 (continued)

		Cognitive level required (currently): Comprehension Application Analysis Synthesis		Obj F: Preparation for curricular selection Obj G: Emphasize reliability, validity, accuracy authority, timeliness, point of view/bias of information Obj H: Emphasize the need to compare/contrast information in different sources
ELD-300- Teaching Math, N-8 (*Junior level*)	*	**Course description**: *"This course focuses on the teaching of mathematics that is developmentally appropriate for students from nursery to grade eight. In keeping with ACET, NAEYC, and NCTM Standards, emphasis is placed on planning for and implementing an integrated curriculum approach, discovery learning, hands-on experience, theme cycles, use of technology, and traditional and non-traditional assessment strategies. Field experiences will consist of classroom observations and teaching individuals and/or small groups of students."* **Assignment**: Develop a mathematics curriculum for K-5 supported by research and resources. **Information Literacy Objectives** (currently): A, B, C, D, E, G, H, I **Cognitive level required** (currently): Comprehension Application Analysis Synthesis	**Information Literacy Objectives** (required): A, B, C, D, E, F, G (Analysis-Synthesis level), H (Analysis-Synthesis level), I **Cognitive level required**: Knowledge Comprehension Application Analysis Synthesis	**Information Literacy skills currently taught**: Obj A: Education indexed databases (professional literature including education journals and ERIC documents) **Reinforcement of skills needed**: A, G, I **Teaching Improvements needed**: Obj A: (expand): Utilize: book catalogs Obj B: Emphasize knowledge production of curricular resources Obj C: Emphasize various library collections available Obj D: Emphasize use of the school library media specialist Obj E: Emphasize sources for classroom curricular resource support Obj F: Preparation for curricular selection Obj G: Emphasize reliability, validity, accuracy authority, timeliness, point of view/bias of information Obj H: Emphasize the need to compare/contrast information in different sources
ELD-300- Teaching Science, Social Studies & the Arts (*Junior level*)	Opportunity	**Course description**: *"This course focuses on methods and materials of instruction in science, social studies, and the arts that are developmentally appropriate for students in preschool through grade eight. This course will incorporate the knowledge and professional attitudes put forth by the National Council for the Social Studies, the American Association for the Advancement of Science, National Art Association, and the Music Educators National Conference. Emphasis is placed on integrated curriculum, hands-on-experiences, theme cycles, unit planning, and traditional and nontraditional assessment strategies. Field experience will consist of observation and analysis of a unit of study over*	**Information Literacy Objectives** (required): A, B, C, D, E, F, G (Analysis-Synthesis level), H (Analysis-Synthesis level), I **Cognitive level required**: Knowledge Comprehension Application Analysis Synthesis	**Information Literacy skills currently taught**: NA (Opportunity) **Reinforcement of skills needed**: A, G, I **Teaching Improvements needed**: NA (opportunity)

Figure 5.4 (continued)

		time in at least one field site as well as continued teaching of lessons to individual and/or small groups of children." **Assignment**: Develop lesson and unit plans that include appropriate resources, teaching and assessment strategies. Includes annotated bibliography of selected resources. **Information Literacy Objectives** *(currently)*: A, B, C, D, E, G, H, I **Cognitive level required** *(currently)*: Comprehension Application Analysis Synthesis		
EDU-400-Student Teaching & Seminar *(Senior level)*	Opportunity	**Course description**: *"A full-time program for seniors providing practical teaching experience in an accredited elementary or secondary school. Under the direct supervision of the cooperating teacher, student teachers are responsible for the planning of lessons and for teaching in their areas of specialization and for developing a high level of teaching competency. Supervisors from [the university] observe the student teachers at work, confer with the cooperating teachers and student teachers, and evaluate the growth of the student teachers throughout the internship period. Special topics are considered in seminars held in conjunction with student teaching. These topics include school health and substance abuse, school law, teacher certification and placement, classroom management, mainstreaming, professionalism, and other topics deemed appropriate by the faculty and student teachers."* **Assignment**: Support course assignments with professional reading. **Information Literacy Objectives** *(currently)*: A, B, C, D, E, G, I **Cognitive level required** *(currently)*: Comprehension Application Analysis	*Information Literacy Objectives* (required): A, B, C, D, E, F, G (Evaluation level), H (Evaluation level), I *Cognitive level required*: Comprehension Application Analysis Synthesis Evaluation	**Information Literacy skills currently taught**: NA (opportunity) **Reinforcement of skills needed**: A, B, C, D, E, F, G (Evaluation level), H (Evaluation level), I **Teaching Improvements needed**: NA (opportunity)

Figure 5.4 (continued)

experience that students in the teacher preparation program tend to limit their use of resources to journal articles, not books. While this is the most appropriate source type for many assignments, there are certainly many opportunities to utilize books to support research assignments.

We identified the specific sequence of skills to be taught and reinforced at each level (from sophomore to junior to senior levels). We noted skill reinforcement and teaching improvements to be made in our teaching for each course. With this information, we were in a position to meet with the chairperson of the Teacher Preparation Department to discuss our proposal.

Step 7: Additional Preparations for Introducing our Proposal: Developing the Curriculum Outline

There are many ways that the library supports its information literacy program, including the provision of instructional materials on the library's Web page. The librarian shares the responsibility of teaching the skills with the faculty in the discipline and collaboration for this process needs to take place. Here were some of our initial suggestions for the librarian's role in teaching the sequenced information literacy skill development for students in the teacher preparation program.

Pre-disciplinary Skill Development (Freshman Level). At our institution, the skills identified for freshman-level mastery have been adapted from the ACRL Standards (ACRL, 2000). Programmatic assessment of these skills has taken place at our institution over a four-year period (Warner, in press). As part of the instruction, which occurs in the required Research Writing course, students are introduced to an online information literacy search skills tutorial and to an additional tutorial providing tips for evaluating information on the "free" Web. These are made available to the students from the Instructional Services link on the libraries' Web page. The search skills tutorial introduces students to skills needed for searching for books and articles and includes an introduction to developing effective search statements (using Boolean logic, truncation, nesting, and incorporation of controlled vocabulary). While some libraries also include computer competency skills as a part of their instruction, this sequence assumes that those skills have been mastered within the Introduction to Computing course required within our core curriculum. Following are the basic skills (see Figure 5.5) that the students should master by the completion of the freshman level.

Introductory Teacher Preparation Level (Sophomore Level). A curriculum will be developed based on an outline for a bibliographic and information literacy sequence for students in the teacher preparation program. An abbreviated version of such a curriculum outline is incorporated here. The following information literacy objectives will be taught at this level: A, G (knowledge level), I. Even though most of the required courses in the teacher preparation program are receiving information literacy instruction, there are two courses that stood out as obvious opportunities for providing the sequenced instruction: the introductory-level Cohort Seminar and the senior-level Student Teaching Seminar.

The recommended teacher preparation information literacy sequence will begin either as a part of the Cohort Seminar or as required workshop(s) for students in the sophomore-level courses. If the workshop option is selected, multiple sections can be offered to accommodate all students. The workshops will be staggered throughout the

Standard One: The information literate student determines the nature and extent of the information needed.

Objective A: Students will identify a variety of types and formats of potential sources of information.
Skill: Utilizing the online catalog (books)
> *Identifies the need for books to fill the information need (knowledge level).*
> *Identifies the online catalog as the access point for identifying relevant books in the institution's library and in other libraries (comprehension level).*
> *Demonstrates the ability to perform a simple search to select a book using the online catalog (application level).*

Skill: Utilizing reference sources
> *Identifies the reference sources as a potential or appropriate source of information (knowledge level).*
> *Locates reference sources to fill the information need (comprehension level).*
> *Utilizes reference sources (application level).*

Skill: Utilizing indexed subscription databases
> *Recognizes the difference between subscription databases and the "free" World Wide Web (application level).*
> *Identifies the indexed databases as a potential or appropriate source of information (knowledge level).*
> *Locates the appropriate indexed database(s) to fill the information need (comprehension level).*
> *Constructs a search statement appropriate for the indexed database(s) (incorporates appropriate keywords and synonyms, controlled vocabularies when appropriate, Boolean operators, nesting of terms, and truncation) (application level).*

Standard Two: The information literate student accesses needed information effectively and efficiently.

Objective A: Students will recognize controlled vocabularies.
Skill: Identifies controlled vocabulary term(s) used in the indexed databases or the online catalog.
Objective B: Students will illustrate search statements that incorporate appropriate keywords and synonyms, controlled vocabularies (when appropriate), Boolean operators, nesting of terms, and truncation, refining the search statement when necessary.
Objective C: Students will determine the most appropriate resources for accessing needed information.
Objective D: Students will successfully acquire the needed information.
Skill: Locating books and periodicals in the institution's library.
> *Identifies tools for locating books or periodicals (knowledge level).*
> *Explains the difference between location tools (e.g., online catalog, find full text journals search) (comprehension level).*
> *Demonstrates the ability to locate a book or periodical in the library (application level).*

Standard Three: The information literate student evaluates information and its sources critically and incorporates selected information into his or her knowledge base and value system.

Objective A: Students will judge the value of a resource by noting its reliability, validity, accuracy, authority, timeliness, point of view or bias.

Standard Four: The information literate student, individually or as a member of a group, uses information effectively to accomplish a specific purpose.

Objective A: Students will assemble the information gathered and create a product.

Standard Five: The information literate student understands many of the economic, legal, and social issues surrounding the use of information and accesses and uses information ethically and legally.

Objective A: Students will appropriately cite their sources.

Figure 5.5 Freshman, 100-Level Information Literacy Skills.

semester to coordinate with the assignments and to accommodate all of the students. The location of the workshops will rotate between the library and the education resource center, as appropriate, so that students will be exposed to relevant sources in both locations.

Course-integrated instruction will continue to occur. The purpose for the additional presence of information literacy in the Cohort Seminar (or workshop) will be to provide consistent instruction of the recommended objectives for this level while providing the time for all of the students to rehearse their skills on multiple occasions and for multiple assignments. Specific field-study related assignments will be addressed within the workshops with recommended resources introduced. The hands-on workshops will provide an opportunity for students to rehearse their information literacy skills while researching sources for their assignments with the support of a librarian.

Librarians will develop an information literacy rubric to align with the assessment rubric being used by the Department of Teacher Preparation to assess the INTASC Standards. The rubric will identify proficiency levels by the conceptual framework areas of commitment, knowledge, reflection, and professionalism. The rubric will be introduced to students at the introductory level.

Students at this level should have completed the freshman-level information literacy requirements identified in the institution's core curriculum or general education requirements. The freshman-level skills should be reinforced at all levels.

To support **Objective A**, we note the literature (see Figure 5.6) to be introduced.

Intermediate Teacher Preparation Level (Junior Level). Course-embedded library instruction will continue to be provided. In addition, multiple staggered (required), hands-on information literacy workshops will be provided that are coordinated with specific assignments in the junior-level courses. The objectives (A, G *at the knowledge level*, and I) that were taught at the introductory level will be reinforced at the intermediate level. Objective G will be developed to the analysis/synthesis level. The objectives introduced at the intermediate level will be Objectives B, C, D, E, F, and H (analysis-synthesis level).

To support **Objectives B, C, D, E, F, and H**, teacher preparation majors will be introduced to knowledge production and representative curricular literature for grades P-12. This will be a coordinated effort between the librarians and the staff of the education resource center in conjunction with the school media center librarian at the site of the student's field placement. Students will also become familiar with the collections available at their public libraries.

It is essential that the teacher preparation students be exposed to the literature published for students in grades P-12 so that they will be prepared to select textbooks and to extend the curriculum with quality literature. This, of course, includes both print and Web production of curricular and supplemental resources. Teacher preparation students also need to be able to understand, analyze, evaluate, synthesize, compare/contrast the content and format of resources, noting the reliability, validity, accuracy, authority, timeliness, point of view, and bias of the content. These skills will be required of them for textbook selection alone.

They need a solid exposure to the variety of content of picture books, including those offering math, history, and language support. Juvenile and young adult literature provides a variety of support for the curriculum, including classic literature, poetry, biography, and historical fiction. There is also an abundance of resource support (both print and electronic) at all levels for the sciences. Computer software exists at every level

---

Primary literature

Education Theories

Education Statements

  Nation at Risk

Education law

  National:

  Brown et al. versus Board of Education

  Education for All Children Act

  State:

  [State] Special Education Code

Education Policies

  Certification requirements (State)

Education Standards

  National:

  Exceptional Children: Council for Exceptional Children Standards (http://www.cec.sped.org/Content/NavigationMenu/ProfessionalDevelopment/ProfessionalStandards)

  Language Arts: National Council of Teachers of English (NCTE): The list of standards for the English language (http://www.ncte.org/about/over/standards)

  Mathematics: National Council of Teachers of Mathematics: Principles and Standards for School Mathematics (http://standards.nctm.org)

  Social Studies: National Council for the Social Studies (NCSS) Standards and Position Statements (http://www.ncss.org/standards)

  Science: National Science Education Standards (http://books.nap.edu/html/nses/overview.html)

  The Arts: National Standards for Arts Education (developed by Consortium of National Arts Education Associations, through a grant administered by National Association for Music Education) (http://artsedge.Kennedy-center.org/teach/standards.cfm

  Information Literacy: American Association of School Librarians (AASL) Position Statements (http://www.ala.org/ala/aasl/aaslproftools/positionstatements/aaslposition.cfm) AND Blueprint for Collaboration (AASL/ACRL, 2000) (http://www.ala.org/ala/acrl/acrlpubs/whitepapers/acrlaaslblueprint.cfm) AND Information Power Standards (AASL/AECT) (http://www.ala.org/acrl/ilcomstan.html)

  Foreign Language: Standards for Foreign Language Learning (http://www.actfl.org/i4 a/pages/index.cfm?pageid=3324)

  School Counseling: National Standards for School Counseling Programs of the American School Counselor Association (ASCA)

  State:

  [State] Information literacy requirements

  Interstate New Teacher Assessment and Support Consortium (INTASC) Model Standards for Beginning Teacher Licensing, Assessment and Development: A Resource for State Dialogue (http://www.ccsso.org/content/pdfs/corestrd.pdf)

  [State] Department of Education Core Curriculum Content Standards and Frameworks

  [State] Board of Education English Language Proficiency Standards

Education government organizations

  Department of Education

    National Center for Education Statistics

Education accrediting organizations

  Middle States Commission on Higher Education

  NCATE

Education associations

  National Association for the Education of Young Children

  The Council for Exceptional Children (http://www.cec.sped.org/ab/student.htm)

  IRA/NAEYC (http://www.naeyc.org)

Figure 5.6 Representative Primary, Secondary, and Tertiary Literature in Support of Objective A (Knowledge Production for the Professional Development of the Teacher Preparation Profession).

Secondary literature

Books (monographs)
Textbooks
Anthologies
Peer-reviewed education journal articles
Conference papers
Dissertations
Quality lesson plans
Curriculum models
Standardized examinations and statistics
    National
    Nation's Report Card, National Assessment of Educational Progress (NAEP)
    California Achievement Test
    State

Tertiary Literature

Hybrid tools:
    Education encyclopedias
        Encyclopedia of Education
        Encyclopedia of American Education
    Education histories
Fact tools:
    Statistical sources
    Common Core of Data
    Condition of Education
    Digest of Education Statistics
    Projections of Education Statistics
    Schools and Staffing Survey
    Education handbooks
    Dictionaries
    Directories
    Almanacs
    Biographical sets
Guides:
    to reference books
    to education literature
Finding Tools:
    Education Subject Guide provided at the library's home page
    Bibliographies (citations, essays)
    Education Indexes & Abstracts (e.g., *ERIC, Education Index, Buros Institute: Index to Mental Measurements Yearbooks*)
        Controlled vocabulary
        Thesauri
    Relevant interdisciplinary Indexes & Abstracts (e.g., *PsycINFO, PsycARTICLES*, major national newspapers)
    Catalogs
        Library of Congress Classification System
        Library of Congress Subject Headings
        Education Library catalogs
    Education Web pages

Figure 5.6 (continued)

to offer support for the curriculum. In addition, teacher preparation students should be aware of the reference sources, periodicals, and academic databases available to students in their P-12 libraries.

Advanced Teacher Preparation Level (Senior Level, during Student Teaching Seminar). Librarians will consult with the students as a group at least twice during the semester to reinforce the objectives introduced earlier (Objectives A, B, C, D, E, F, G, H, and I). Individual consultations for research support will also be provided. Librarians will provide research logs to be completed by the students (for an example, see Figure 4.2).

Step 8: Shared Responsibility for Assessment

Knowing that the students are learning the skills is the ultimate satisfaction for the teacher and the learner. Here are our assessment recommendations.

> *Introductory Level*. There will be three separate assessments that involve the student, the librarian, and the teacher preparation faculty. A rubric will be developed based on the information literacy objectives (for an example, see Figure 10.5). Students will reflect on their research experiences by completing a (required) self-assessment, and, using the rubric, they will identify their proficiency levels reached. The librarians working with the introductory-level students will also complete the rubric for each student and both will compare their assessments. Students will indicate on a separate checklist those skills that they need to develop. Based on the success of the students' research for the sophomore-level assignments, the teacher preparation faculty will provide the librarians with recommendations for information literacy skill development needed at the intermediate level.
>
> *Intermediate level*. Librarians will build upon the recommendations of the teacher preparation faculty (from the sophomore-level courses) and the student-identified skills that need development. They will then receive similar feedback from the faculty teaching junior-level courses.
>
> Students will again reflect on their research experiences by completing a (required) self-assessment, identifying the information literacy skills on the rubric that they have learned and by indicating on a checklist those skills that they need to develop. The librarians will do the same and compare the assessments of the student and the librarian.
>
> *Advanced level*. Preliminary research logs will be submitted to the librarians who will consult individually with students and provide research recommendations. A final research log will be submitted to the librarians who will identify the proficiency levels reached according to the information literacy rubric.

REFERENCES

American Association of School Librarians (AASL) and Association of College and Research Libraries (ACRL). "Blueprint for Collaboration." (2000). http://www.ala.org/ala/acrl/acrlpubs/whitepapers/acrlaaslblueprint.cfm (accessed March 13, 2008).

American Association of School Librarians (AASL) and Association for Educational Communications and Technology (AECT). *Information Power: Building Partnerships for Learning.* Chicago, IL: American Library Association, 1998.

Association of College & Research Libraries (ACRL). *Information Literacy Competency Standards for Higher Education*. (2000). http://www.ala.org/ala/acrl/acrlstandards/informationliteracycompetency.cfm (accessed March 13, 2008).

Carr, Jo Ann, and Ilene F. Rockman. "Information-Literacy Collaboration: A Shared Responsibility." *American Libraries* 34(8) (2003): 52–54.

Council of Chief State School Officers. *Model Standards for Beginning Teacher Licensing, Assessment, and Development: A Resource for State Dialogue*. Washington, DC: Council of Chief State School Officers, 1992. http://www.ccsso.org/content/pdfs/corestrd.pdf (accessed December 11, 2007).

Educational Media Association of New Jersey (EMAnj). "School Library Media Curriculum Template." (2000). http://www.emanj.org/documents/Template.pdf (accessed March 14, 2008).

Eisenberg, Michael B., and Robert E. Berkowitz. *Information Problem-solving: The Big 6 Skills Approach to Library and Information Skills*. Norwood, NJ: Ablex Publishing Corp., 1990.

Kleiman, Neil Scott. "Building a Highway to Higher Ed: How Collaborative Efforts are Changing Education in America." Center for an Urban Future (2001). http://www.nycfuture.org/content/reports/report_view.cfm?repkey=10 (accessed June 16, 2007).

National Council of Teachers of English and the International Reading Association (NCTE/IRA). *Standards for the English Language Arts*. http://www.ncte.org/about/over/standards/110846.htm (accessed September 27, 2007).

Rider University. *Strategic Plan 2005–2010*. Lawrenceville, NJ: Rider University, 2005.

Warner, Dorothy. "Programmatic Assessment of Information Literacy Skills Using Rubrics." *Journal on Excellence in College Teaching* (in press).

ADDITIONAL READINGS

O'Brien, Nancy Patricia. *Education: A Guide to Reference and Information Sources* (2nd ed.). Englewood, CO: Libraries Unlimited, 2000.

Shinew, Dawn M., and Scott Walter. *Information Literacy Instruction for Educators: Professional Knowledge for an Information Age*. New York: The Haworth Information Press, 2003 (*see especially the chapter by Corey M. Johnson and Lorena O'English, "Information Literacy in Pre-Service Teacher Preparation: An Annotated Bibliography," pp. 129–139*).

6

Recommended Sequence for Bibliographic and Information Literacy: Communication and Journalism

Communication programs vary tremendously. Some programs are rooted in business departments, others are combined with journalism, others are combined with film, and others are focused on the mass media, thus determining the focus of the program. Regardless of the various curricula, there are consistent information literacy requirements necessary for effective and accurate communication in the written, aural, verbal, and multiple visual environments of this field (including television, film, and Web communications). The approach given here provides a core curriculum with offerings for majors in the optional tracks of multimedia communication, radio and television, speech and interpersonal communication, and journalism (including news and editorial journalism and public relations).

Students in this major will be required to be facile "free" Web information-seekers. For a communication major, the information seeking may begin on the Web and then take the route of verifying the accuracy of the information from recognized professional sources.

ASSESSMENT GOALS OF THE COMMUNICATION AND JOURNALISM DEPARTMENT

These model assessment goals and objectives for communication and journalism were "based on a body of knowledge and skills necessary for entering the various professions in the communication and journalism field. These are based on established standards of various professional and scholarly organizations in the communication discipline" (Brown and Xia, 2007). Learning objectives for students with a major in communication and journalism include being able to "identify significant individuals and organizations and their contributions to the communication field" (Objective 1); being able to "explain and apply major concepts and theories in the communication field" (Objective 2); being able to "engage in effective written and oral communication activities" (Objective 3); understanding and being able to apply "appropriate legal and ethical standards for professional communicators" (Objective 4); understanding "how the media function currently and in the past as organizations and as institutions in society" (Objective 5) (Brown and Xia, 2007, reprinted with permission from Rider University).

LITERATURE REVIEW: STANDARDS, BEST PRACTICES, AND DEPARTMENTAL TEXTBOOKS

Standards

A review was done of the Professional Values and Competencies of the Curriculum and Instruction Standard (#2) of the Accrediting Standards of the Accrediting Council on Education in Journalism and Mass Communications (ACEJMC). Most of the professional values and competencies of this standard require an effective grounding in bibliographic and information literacy skills. The library recognized the need to support those in **bold** within the standards (ahead). The accreditation requirement for Standard 2, Curriculum and Instruction, is that "the unit provides a curriculum and instruction that enable students to learn the knowledge, competencies and values the Council defines for preparing students to work in a diverse global and domestic society." For the Professional Values and Competencies, "the Accrediting Council on Education in Journalism and Mass Communications requires that, irrespective of their particular specialization, all graduates should be aware of certain core values and competencies and be able to: **understand and apply the principles and laws of freedom of speech and press, including the right to dissent, to monitor and criticize power, and to assemble and petition for redress of grievances; demonstrate an understanding of the history and role of professionals and institutions in shaping communications; demonstrate an understanding of the diversity of groups in a global society in relationship to communications; understand concepts and apply theories in the use and presentation of images and information; demonstrate an understanding of professional ethical principles and work ethically in pursuit of truth, accuracy, fairness and diversity; think critically, creatively and independently; conduct research and evaluate information by methods appropriate to the communications professions in which they work;** write correctly and clearly in forms and styles appropriate for the communications professions, audiences and purposes they serve; **critically evaluate their own work and that of others for accuracy and fairness, clarity, appropriate style and grammatical correctness;** apply basic numerical and statistical concepts; apply tools and technologies appropriate for the communications professions in which they work" (ACEJMC, 2004, reprinted with permission).

Best Practices

Humboldt State University Library has developed ten information competencies for the journalism professional based upon competencies expected by journalism educators and professionals in the industry. Our library, which distinguishes between information literacy and computer literacy, selected seven competencies to address and, within those seven competencies we chose specific objectives to support (our selections are in **bold** as shown in Figure 6.1). The Humboldt State University Library Web page provides useful links within each competency category (http://library.humboldt.edu/~ccm/fingertips/journal1.htm).

- **Writing Competencies** are routinely identified as critical to the accuracy, clarity, credibility, and reliability of a story. Attention must be given to the technical skills of writing as well as the intended audience and format. Stories written for a newspaper in the United States require a different approach when placed on the Web for a more international audience.
  - Ability to write clearly using proper grammar, spelling, and punctuation
  - Knowledge and use of broad vocabulary
  - Ability to recognize and write a lead paragraph
  - **Ability to properly credit sources**
  - Ability to use appropriate tools for writing
- **Oral Performance Competencies** are critical to promoting understanding, eliciting meaningful responses, and establishing confidence and trust. Interview skills should be developed to explore the appropriate techniques and methods to be utilized when interviewing children, ethnic groups, trauma victims, etc. The nuances of public speaking should also be addressed.
  - Ability to communicate effectively in standard English
  - **Ability to apply basic interview techniques across various cultures and age groups**
  - **Ability to formulate effective questions**
  - Ability to speak effectively in public forums
- **Research and Investigative Competencies** must be honed to prepare a well developed, accurate story or to identify potential topics.
  - **Awareness of and ability to utilize print reference sources available in most libraries**
  - **Awareness of and ability to utilize online virtual reference sources**
  - **Awareness of and an ability to conduct public records searches**
- Broad-based Knowledge Competencies include the need for a basic knowledge of the fundamentals of economics, statistics, mathematics, history, science, health care, business, and governmental structure is critical for entry-level professionals. Once practicing it is the responsibility of the professional to continue lifelong learning and further expansion of the existing knowledge base.
  - Arts & Humanities
  - Business
  - Economics
  - Ethnic Studies
  - Health & Health Care
  - History
  - Mathematics
  - Political Science & Government
  - Science
  - Statistics
- **Web-Based Competencies** are no longer optional. Proficient use of the Internet, e-mail, mailing lists, newsgroups, and the ability to provide news in an on-demand format have become increasingly important in today's society. These competencies are mandatory for professionals to remain in the lead of breaking news and information. It is critical, however, that professionals also be able to judge the authenticity, accuracy, and reliability of the plethora of information available on the Web.
  - **Ability to effectively navigate the Web utilizing the most appropriate search tools**
  - Ability to utilize e-mail
  - **Working knowledge of listservs, mailing lists, and newsgroups within the discipline**
  - **Awareness of the need to evaluate Internet information**
  - **Ability to objectively evaluate Internet information**
  - Ability to design a simple Web page using html
- Audio Visual Competencies
  - Ability to operate a 35 mm still camera
  - Ability to operate a video camera
  - Ability to scan photographs into a computer
  - Ability to operate an audio tape recorder

Figure 6.1 Humboldt State University Library Information Competencies for the Journalism Professional.
Source: Yancheff, Catherine, Librarian, Humboldt State University. "Information Competencies for the Journalism Professional." Arcata, CA: Humboldt State University Library (2005). http://library.humboldt.edu/~ccm/fingertips/journal1. html (accessed March 14, 2008). Reprinted with permission.

- Skill-Based Computer Application Competencies will be necessary in creating stories. Word processing, database development (especially useful for investigative reports), and multimedia applications, including Pagemaker, Quark XPress, and Printshop, etc., will enhance the journalist's workflow as well as the final story.
  - Ability to utilize both Macintosh and PC platforms
  - Ability to use a word processing program beyond the introductory level
  - Ability to create a simple database
  - Ability to use a desktop publisher
  - Ability to use a desktop scanner
- **Ethics Competencies** continue to be a concern to the profession and are discussed at length in various forums.
  - **Awareness of the professional code of conduct**
  - **Awareness of ethical considerations in making value choices**
  - **Understanding of fallacies and how to avoid them.**
  - **Understanding of plagiarism**
- **Legal Competencies** include the Freedom of Information Act (FOIA), the First Amendment, and copyright issues. **Familiarity with these issues and their impact on the profession and society are critical to the profession**.
  - **Awareness and understanding of the Freedom of Information Act**
  - **Awareness and understanding of the First Amendment**
  - **Awareness and understanding of the U. S. Copyright Law**
- **Career Competencies** will remain an important feature throughout the career of a journalism professional. Useful links with valuable information are available for help in finding an internship or for guidance in resume development for that next professional move. Work place skills include everything from time-management and diligent work habits to teamwork and maintaining a positive attitude. Other career aspects may include managerial components such as market and audience analysis, running an assignment desk, producing and editing. Professional Networking as with any profession, is critical to staying abreast of the current trends, issues, and recognizing "who's who."
  - **Ability to develop a professional resume**
  - **Awareness of internships and how to locate them**
  - **Awareness of professional "job" banks and resources for seeking placement**
  - Awareness and understanding of time-management skills
  - **Awareness of professional associations and networks**
  - Awareness and understanding of managerial issues including market and audience analysis, coordinating the assignment desk, and producing and editing the news.

Figure 6.1 (continued)

Review of Departmental Textbooks

Textbooks for both the required courses and for some relevant electives were examined to determine student exposure to research skills. One text (Griffin, 2006) used in a required introductory public speaking course includes two research-related chapters: Gathering Support Materials (Chapter 6) and Developing and Supporting your Ideas (Chapter 7). Chapter 6 provides a sample research inventory (p. 117), which prompts the researcher to identify examples, statistics, testimony, and definitions for the speech. It then prompts the researcher to list the "kinds of sources [that the audience] will find trustworthy" (p. 117) and then to identify specific types of sources for locating specific types of information. Another textbook stresses verifying the accuracy of the information discovered. These textbooks are exemplary of the shared responsibility for the teaching of information literacy skills. For a communication and journalism major, source evaluation is paramount in the research process and our role is to strengthen that evaluation skill.

Objective A: Students will understand knowledge production for the communication and journalism professions, including the abilities to recognize and utilize primary, secondary, and tertiary sources of information and be able to distinguish among news, scholarly, and professional sources of information. [Graduated skill development beginning at the FRESHMAN YEAR, performing at the application level; SOPHOMORE YEAR, performing at the analysis level; JUNIOR YEAR, performing at the synthesis level; SENIOR YEAR, performing at the evaluation level] [Supports Communication & Journalism Assessment Objectives #1, 2, 5]

Objective B: Students will identify and utilize standard communication and journalism sources for researching significant individuals and organizations and their contributions to the communication field. These will include communication and journalism reference sources (e.g., both print and electronic encyclopedias, dictionaries, biographical sources), book catalogs, subject indexes to communication and journalism journals (both print and electronic), relevant interdisciplinary indexes to professional journals (both print and electronic), public records, information produced by government agencies, relevant Web sites of interest to the communication and journalism profession, including internship and career sites. Students will distinguish between standard professional communication and journalism sources and interdisciplinary sources relevant to the profession. [Graduated skill development beginning at the FRESHMAN YEAR, performing at the comprehension level; SOPHOMORE YEAR, performing at the application level; JUNIOR YEAR, performing at the analysis and synthesis levels; SENIOR YEAR, performing at the evaluation level] [Supports Communication & Journalism Assessment Objectives #1, 2, 5]

Objective C: Students will be able to locate information including examples, narratives, statistics, testimony, and definitions to support their products (e.g., speeches, papers, articles, interview questions). [Cognitive level: application] [FRESHMAN YEAR] [Supports Communication & Journalism Assessment Objectives #1, 2, 5]

Objective D: Students will understand how government information is organized, identify the need to access government information, and utilize information from municipal, state, federal, or international government sources. [Graduated skill development beginning at the SOPHOMORE YEAR, performing at the application level; JUNIOR YEAR, performing at the analysis and synthesis levels; SENIOR YEAR, performing at the evaluation level] [Supports Communication & Journalism Assessment Objectives #3, 4]

Objective E: Students will be able to compare/contrast information from multiple sources (regardless of format) in order to ensure the accuracy of information used. [Graduated skill development beginning at the FRESHMAN YEAR, performing at the knowledge level; SOPHOMORE YEAR, performing at the comprehension level; JUNIOR YEAR, performing at the application and analysis levels; SENIOR YEAR, performing at the synthesis and evaluation levels] [Supports Communication & Journalism Assessment Objectives #3, 4]

Objective F: Students will judge the value of a resource (regardless of format) by noting its reliability, validity, accuracy, authority, timeliness, point of view or bias. [Graduated skill development beginning at the FRESHMAN YEAR, performing at the comprehension level; SOPHOMORE YEAR, performing at the application level; JUNIOR YEAR, performing at the analysis and synthesis levels, SENIOR YEAR, performing at the evaluation level] [Supports Communication & Journalism Assessment Objectives #3, 4]

Objective G: Students will appropriately cite their sources. [Cognitive level: application] [FRESHMAN YEAR] [Supports Communication & Journalism Assessment Objectives #3, 4]

Figure 6.2 Information Literacy Objectives for Communication and Journalism.

BIBLIOGRAPHIC AND INFORMATION LITERACY OBJECTIVES

From these sources, in combination with the initial curriculum map developed for the department, several bibliographic and information literacy objectives (see Figure 6.2) were developed to support the department's assessment goals.

REVIEWING THE CURRICULUM MAP

All students, regardless of their track specialization, are required to take a core sequence of courses. Four of these courses are taken in the first year of the major.

In addition to the communication core, each student must fulfill requirements in their selected track. The curriculum map (ahead) enabled us to visualize the sequence most effectively and identify precisely what should be taught to students at each stage of the curricular sequence. Our initial map was produced in Excel and identified all courses (including electives) available for the major, which track requirement the course filled, whether library instruction had been taught, assignment details, professors scheduled to teach, and the total number of sections taught over the past four years. This abbreviated model describes the core courses, the *current* information literacy skills covered in each, and the information literacy skills recommended (*required*) for the level of the sequence. Unless otherwise noted, the 100-level courses are freshman-level courses, the 200-level and the 300-level courses are open to sophomores and juniors, and the 400-level courses are open to juniors and seniors, with the exception of the Senior Seminar (seniors only). While there are additional courses offered for each track, we identified those that were nonproduction courses and then identified the eligible course selections for each track. This way we were able to identify those courses for information literacy instruction (see Figure 6.3) that would reach students in the majority of the tracks.

As noted with the teacher preparation sequence, one must look more closely at each information literacy objective to determine how completely the objective is being both taught and then learned. Each objective has many elements and, for each of the courses, we needed to look closely at exactly what we were teaching and how we might deepen the instruction that we were already providing. We also needed to examine each track and ensure that there was a complete sequence for each major.

Although we had noted the objectives that must be taught at the freshman year, we needed to be specific about what had to be taught to sophomores and juniors so that we were both reinforcing and developing the students' skills. And we then had to determine precisely what we expected all students, regardless of the track selected, to be able to perform at the conclusion of the senior year. At this point, we developed a curriculum outline.

CURRICULUM OUTLINE OF BIBLIOGRAPHIC AND INFORMATION LITERACY LEARNING OBJECTIVES FOR MAJORS IN COMMUNICATION AND JOURNALISM

Shared Responsibility for Teaching the Information Literacy Skills

While developing the curriculum outline we realized the need to provide more specific bibliographic and information literacy skills to different tracks. For example, the Speech and Interpersonal Communication track offered several courses that were exclusive to majors in that track. This affected how we were to deliver the instructional sequence.

We recommended that seminars (to be called Information Literacy Seminars) be offered to run parallel to the courses, while continuing course-integrated information literacy instruction where necessary. At the freshman, 100-level year, since four of the required courses are taken, all majors will be required to take the Introductory Information Literacy Freshman Seminar (which will be offered multiple times during the first two weeks of the semester to accommodate student schedules). The information taught in this seminar will be reinforced within each course where assignment-related instruction occurs. The instruction in the introductory seminar will be specific to the needs of communication and journalism majors and distinct from the instruction in the general education requirement that students will simultaneously be fulfilling in their Research Writing course.

COURSE (Bold designates core courses required for all majors in Communication and Journalism)	Course Description (*Source for descriptions*: Rider University. *Undergraduate Catalog 06/07.* Lawrenceville, NJ: Rider University, 2006.)	Information Literacy Objectives Identified in Syllabi (*Currently*)	Cognitive level (*Currently*)	Recommended Information Literacy Objectives (*Required for the Identified Sequence Level*)	Cognitive level (*Required*)
COM-103- Introduction to Communication Studies: Theory & Practice (*Freshman year*)	*Course description:* "Provides a foundation for the study in the field of human communication. The course is designed, but not limited to, helping first year communication and journalism majors gain a broad understanding about the discipline while introducing them to fundamental communication theories, principles, concepts, terms, and issues." *Assignment:* Group project requiring research.	*Information Literacy Objectives (currently):* A, B, C, F (Application level), G	*Cognitive level (currently) required:* Application	*Information Literacy Objectives (required):* A (Application level), B (Comprehension level), C, E (Knowledge level), F (Comprehension level), G	*Cognitive levels required:* Knowledge, Comprehension, Application
COM-104- Speech Communication (*Freshman year*)	*Course description:* "Examines basic communication theories and concepts. Various genres of oral communication and extemporaneous and impromptu forms of delivery are studied. Students research, prepare, and deliver speeches that are then used as the focal point for the discussion of effective speaking and listening. A number of speeches are videotaped." *Assignment:* Research to support speeches.	*Information Literacy Objectives (currently):* B, C, F, G	*Cognitive level (currently) required:* Application	*Information Literacy Objectives (required):* A (Application level), B (Comprehension level), C, E (Knowledge level) (Application level), F (Comprehension level), G	*Cognitive level required:* Knowledge, Comprehension, Application
COM-105-Mass Media Communication (*Freshman year*)	*Course description:* "Provides a detailed investigation and analysis into the nature, history, scope, adequacy, and limitations of mass communication and examines the reciprocal influence of the media on culture and society." *Assignment:* Research paper; presentation.	*Information Literacy Objectives (currently):* B (Knowledge level)	*Cognitive level (currently) required:* Knowledge	*Information Literacy Objectives (required):* A (Application level), B (Comprehension level), C, E (Knowledge level), F (Comprehension level), G	*Cognitive level required:* Knowledge, Comprehension, Application

Figure 6.3 Core Communication and Journalism Courses for all Tracks: Communication Major Tracks: Multi-Media Communication; Radio and Television; Speech and Interpersonal Communication; Journalism Major Tracks: News-Editorial Journalism; Public Relations/Journalism.

COM-107-Persuasive Writing for the Media (*Freshman year*)	*Course description:* "Introduces students to interviewing and persuasive writing techniques for print and electronic public relations and advertising formats. Teaches techniques for creating effective digital audio-visual aids and working with digital audio and video." *Assignment:* NA	*Information Literacy Objectives (currently):* NA	*Cognitive level (currently) required:* NA	*Information Literacy Objectives (required):* A (Application level), B (Comprehension level), C, E (Knowledge level), F (Comprehension level), G	*Cognitive level required:* Knowledge, Comprehension, Application
NOTE: For the sophomore year, there are no core requirements for communication and journalism majors as sophomores select courses required for their track.					
COM-301-Communication Law (*Junior, Senior year*)	*Course description:* "Critically examines the legal limits and privileges affecting freedom of expression, especially in publishing, advertising, film, telecasting, and cyberspace. Places particular emphasis on the historical and philosophical foundations of the freedoms and limitations of communication in the United States." *Assignment:* Study questions.	*Information Literacy Objectives (currently):* NA	*Cognitive level (currently) required:* NA	*Information Literacy Objectives (required):* A (Synthesis-Evaluation levels), B (Analysis, Synthesis, Evaluation levels), C, D (Analysis-Synthesis levels), E (Application-Analysis levels), F (Analysis-Synthesis levels), G	*Cognitive level required:* Analysis, Synthesis, & Evaluation
COM-302-Communication Ethics (*Junior, Senior year*)	*Course description:* "Analyzes internal and external pressures on the communication professional including economic, cultural, social, and political pressures, assesses the philosophical and practical basis for responding to such pressures, evaluates contemporary media responses to these pressures, identifies those that are of laudable quality and why, and provides guidance as to how individuals and organizations can think and react ethically. Issues addressed include censorship, confidentiality, conflicts of interests, minority and ethnic groups, privacy, sensationalism, and self-criticism." *Assignment:* Issue debates and case studies.	*Information Literacy Objectives (currently):* NA	*Cognitive level (currently) required:* NA	*Information Literacy Objectives (required):* A (Synthesis-Evaluation levels), B (Analysis, Synthesis, Evaluation levels), C, D (Analysis-Synthesis levels), E (Application-Analysis levels), F (Analysis-Synthesis levels), G	*Cognitive level required:* Analysis, Synthesis, & Evaluation

Figure 6.3 (continued)

COM-400-Senior Seminar in Communication (*Senior year*)	*Course description*: "Utilizes quantitative and qualitative research to investigate current topics in communication. Students conceptualize problems, develop hypotheses, review literature, design appropriate techniques of inquiry, conduct their research, and present their findings orally to the seminar and in writing to the instructor." **Assignment**: Several research projects requiring professional literature. **This pattern would continue for each course in a completed curriculum map.**	*Information Literacy Objectives (currently)*: A (Application level), B (Analysis level), E (Analysis level), F (Analysis level), G	*Cognitive level (currently) required*: Analysis	*Information Literacy Objectives (required)*: A (Evaluation level), B (Evaluation level), C, D (Evaluation level), E (Synthesis-Evaluation levels), F (Evaluation level), G	*Cognitive levels required*: Synthesis, Evaluation

NA = Not available, as information literacy requirements do not currently exist in the assignments for this course. This represents an opportunity to negotiate with the professor(s) to introduce an information literacy requirement.

Figure 6.3 (continued)

Seminars will be offered at the beginning of each year of the sequence. These will be for the purpose of reinforcing the skills learned during the previous year and introducing skills required for the specific year. Several hands-on workshop opportunities will then be offered during each semester. Workshops will be organized by class year so that students taking courses together will be able to support each other's learning needs. We decided also to identify the workshops by major (either communication or journalism) since the information-seeking needs will vary as the students progress through the major. Students will be required to attend two hands-on workshops each semester (in addition to the seminar). During the hands-on workshops, students will receive librarian support for course-specific assignments.

Freshman Year

Freshman Information Literacy Seminar (one two-hour introductory session followed by two required one-hour workshops each semester): The mandatory seminar will be taught parallel to the core courses: COM-103-Introduction to Communication Studies: Theory & Practice; COM-104-Speech Communication; COM-105-Mass Media Communication.

Session #1: This initial seminar will begin with an Introduction to the Information Literacy Objectives. Freshmen will be expected to learn Objective A (application level), Objective B (comprehension level), Objectives C, E (knowledge level), F (comprehension level), & G. Students will also be introduced to the library's Web-based research inventory (Figure 6.6) that they will maintain for all four years of their major. Sources introduced to meet Objectives A & B will be available in a communication and journalism subject guide on the library's Web page and include the following primary, secondary, and tertiary literature (see Figure 6.4).

Primary literature

Communication theories
Communication and Journalism Standards
Communication and Journalism Associations
 Association for Education in Journalism and Mass Communication (http://www.aejmc.org)
 Investigative Reporters and Editors, Inc. (Missouri School of Journalism) (http://www.ire.org)
 National Association of Broadcasters (http://www.nab.org)
 National Newspaper Association (http://www.nna.org)
 Society of Professional Journalists (http://www.spj.org)
 Newspaper Association of America (http://www.naa.org)
 Associated Press (http://www.ap.org)
Internship opportunities
Career opportunities
 Journalismjobs.com (http://www.journalismjobs.com)
Laws
 Freedom of Information Act
 First Amendment
 U. S. Copyright Law
News
 BBC News World Edition (http://news.bbc.co.uk)
 PollingReport. com (An independent, nonpartisan resource on trends in American public opinion) (http://www.pollingreport. com)
 Articles available in newspapers [e.g., accessed via individual Web sites or collectively in databases such as *Factiva*]
 Information produced by government agencies
Public records

Secondary literature

Books (monographs)
Textbooks
Anthologies
Peer-reviewed Communication and Journalism journal articles (scholarly)
 TE: Editor & Publisher: America's Oldest Journal Covering the Newspaper Industry (http://www. editorandpublisher. com)
 Digital Journalist: A Multimedia Magazine for Photojournalism in the Digital Age (University of Texas at Austin) (http://digitaljournalist.org)
 Federal Communications Law Journal (http://www.law.indiana.edu/fclj)
Professional literature
 Mediaweek (http://www.mediaweek. com)
 Articles in business journals [e.g., in the database, *ABI/INFORM*]
 Articles in education journals [e.g., in the database, *ERIC*]
 Articles in sociology journals [e.g., in the database, *Social Sciences Full Text*]
 Articles in psychology journals [e.g., in the database, *PsycINFO* or *PsycARTICLES*]
Conference papers
Dissertations
Quotation books
 Oxford Dictionary of Humorous Quotations

Tertiary literature

Hybrid Tools:
Encyclopedias
 Encyclopedia of American Radio: An A-Z Guide to Radio from Jack Benny to Howard Stern
 Encyclopedia of International Media and Communications
 Encyclopedia of New Media: An Essential Reference to Communication and Technology
 Encyclopedia of Radio
 Encyclopedia of Television
 World Press Encyclopedia: A Survey of Press Systems Worldwide
 Encyclopedia of International Media and Communications

Figure 6.4 Bibliographic Outline.

Encyclopedia of Censorship
Encyclopedia of Communication and Information
Yearbooks
    Broadcasting & Cable Yearbook
    Editor & Publisher International Year Book: The Encyclopedia of the Newspaper Industry
Histories
    History of the Mass Media in the United States
    Swingin' on the Ether Waves: A Chronological History of African Americans in Radio and Television Broadcasting, 1925–1955

Fact Tools:
Statistical sources
    Television & Cable Factbook
    NationMaster.Com ("Where Stats Come Alive!") http://www.nationmaster.com/index.php
Handbooks
    World at Risk: A Global Issues Sourcebook
Dictionaries
Directories
    Burrelle's Media Directory
    O'Dwyer's Directory of Public Relations Firms
Almanacs
    International Television & Video Almanac
Biographical sets
Atlases
    Atlapedia Online (Maps and Country Data) (http://www.atlapedia.com)
Gazetteers

Guides:
Guides to reference books
    Journalism: A Guide to the Reference Literature
Guides to Communication and Journalism literature
Other Guides
    Columbia Guide to Digital Publishing
    Media in Europe
    Associated Press Stylebook and Briefing on Media Law

Finding Tools:
Communication and Journalism Subject Guide provided at the library's home page
Bibliographies (citations, essays)
Subject Specific Indexes & Abstracts (e.g., *Communication Abstracts*, *Communication and Mass Media Complete* [database])
    Controlled vocabulary
Relevant Interdisciplinary Indexes & Abstracts (e.g., *Readers' Guide to Periodical Literature*, *Wilson Omnifile*)
Indexes & Abstracts of Newspaper articles (e.g., the index, *National Newspaper Index*; the database, *Factiva*)
Catalogs
"Free" Web information seeking
    Search engines
    Invisible Web
    Internet Gateway
    Journalism Resources (compiled and edited by Karla Tonella, University of Iowa) (http://bailiwick.lib.uiowa.edu/journalism)
    Overseas Press Club of America: Serving the Interests of Foreign Correspondents since 1939 (http://www.opcofamerica.org)

Figure 6.4 (continued)

Sessions #2 & 3: These hands-on sessions will be held in the library and be co-ordinated with assignments in the COM-103-Introduction to Communication Studies: Theory & Practice; COM-104-Speech Communication; and COM-105-Mass Media Communication courses.

Sophomore Year

Sophomore Information Literacy Seminar (one two-hour seminar followed by two required one-hour workshops each semester): The initial sophomore-year seminar will reinforce the information literacy objectives and reintroduce the library Web-based research inventory that students will continue to maintain. Objectives to be reinforced from the freshman year are Objective A (advancing to the analysis level during the sophomore year; students will responsibly utilize the invisible Web), Objective B (advancing to the application level during the sophomore year), Objective C, Objective E (advancing to the comprehension level during the sophomore year), Objective F (advancing to the application level during the sophomore year), and Objective G. Objective D will be introduced during the sophomore year and is particularly important for the journalism tracks: News-Editorial Journalism and Public Relations.

There are no core requirements for communication and journalism majors during this year as sophomores select courses required for their track. Course-embedded information literacy development will occur in those sophomore-year courses identified that provide opportunities for developing information literacy skills for communication and journalism majors (e. g., COM-201-Communication Theory; COM-204-Advanced Speech; COM-205-Theories of Persuasion; COM-210-News Reporting and Writing; and COM-240-Public Relations). Courses from which students select electives for their specific track are identified in Figure 6.5.

Session #1: Students will participate in an invisible Web workshop and be introduced to Objective D (organization of government information). They will participate in an exercise to emphasize the significance of Objective E (comparing/contrasting information, developed to the comprehension level during the sophomore year) and Objective F (judging the value of a resource, developed to the application level during the sophomore year) for the communication and journalism profession. The exercise will be a modification of the exercises demonstrated by Rouet, Britt et al. (1996); Hynd-Shanahan, Holschuh, and Hubbard (2004); and Schaus (1990).

Sessions #2 & 3: These hands-on sessions will be held in the library and be coordinated with assignments in the COM-201-Communication Theory; COM-204-Advanced Speech; COM-205-Theories of Persuasion; and COM-210-News Reporting and Writing courses.

Junior Year

Junior Information Literacy Seminar (one two-hour seminar followed by two required one-hour workshops each semester): The initial junior-year seminar will reinforce the information literacy objectives and reintroduce the library Web-based research inventory that students will continue to maintain. The core requirements for juniors are: COM-301, Communication Law, and COM-302, Communication Ethics. Objectives reinforced during this academic year will be Objective A (advancing to the synthesis level during the junior year), Objective B (advancing to the analysis and synthesis levels during the junior year), Objective C, Objective D (advancing to the analysis and synthesis levels

Course	Communication Major Track: Multimedia Communication	Communication Major Track: Radio and Television	Communication Major Track: Speech and Interpersonal Communication	Journalism Major Track: News-Editorial Journalism	Journalism Major Track: Public Relations/Journalism
COM-201-Communication Theory	*		*	*	*
COM-204-Advanced Speech	*	*	*	*	*
COM-205-Theories of Persuasion	*	*	*	*	*
COM-210-News Reporting & Writing				*	*
COM-222-Group Communication			*		
COM-233-Writing for Broadcast	*	*	*	*	*
COM-240-Public Relations		*	*	*	*
COM-251-Interpersonal Communication			*		
COM-252-Intercultural Communication			*		
COM-253-Organizational Communication	*	*	*	*	*
COM-291-Documentary Film		*			
COM-322-Argumentation & Debate			*		
COM-323-Oral Interpretation of Literature			*		
COM-353-Nonverbal Communication			*		
COM-391-Communication Criticism			*		
COM-393-International Communication			*		

Figure 6.5 Electives for the Five Communication and Journalism Tracks.
∗ – *May be selected for this track.*

during the junior year; important for both core courses during this year), Objective E (advancing to the application and analysis levels during the junior year), Objective F (advancing to the analysis and synthesis levels during the junior year), and Objective G.

Course-embedded information literacy development will occur in those junior-year courses identified that provide opportunities for developing information literacy skills for communication and journalism majors (e. g., COM-415, Investigative Reporting, for the News-Editorial Journalism track; COM-452, Contemporary Issues in Interpersonal Communication, for the Speech and Interpersonal Communication track).

Session #1: Emphasis in the Junior Information Literacy Seminar will be on re-inforcing and developing further the skills of Objective D (organization of govern-ment information), Objective E (comparing/contrasting information, developed to the application-analysis levels during the junior year) and Objective F (judging the value of a resource, developed to the analysis-synthesis levels during the junior year). An additional exercise will be designed (see sophomore year, session #1) and introduced to develop these skills, which will be reinforced by the communication and journalism professors as they are essential for success in the junior-year core courses, COM-301, Communication Law, and COM-302, Communication Ethics. Students will also partic-ipate in an Advanced Invisible Web Workshop, with content designed to support the Communication Law and Communication Ethics course.

Sessions #2 & 3: These hands-on sessions will be held in the library and be co-ordinated with assignments in the COM-301, Communication Law, and COM-302, Communication Ethics courses.

Senior Year

Senior Information Literacy Seminar (one two-hour seminar followed by two required one-hour workshops each semester): The initial senior-year seminar will reinforce the information literacy objectives and reintroduce the library Web-based research inventory that students will continue to maintain. Objectives A, B, D, E, and F will be developed to the evaluation level while Objectives C and G will be reinforced.

Course-embedded instruction will occur in COM-400, Senior Seminar in Commu-nication (core requirement); COM-415, Investigative Reporting (News-Editorial Jour-nalism track); and COM-452, Contemporary Issues in Interpersonal Communication (Speech and Interpersonal Communication track).

Session #1: Emphasis in the Senior Information Literacy Seminar will be on reinforc-ing and developing further the skills of Objective E (comparing/contrasting information, developed to the synthesis-evaluation levels during the senior year) and Objective F (judging the value of a resource, developed to the evaluation level during the senior year).

Sessions #2 & 3: These hands-on sessions will be held in the library and be coordi-nated with student projects in the Senior Seminar.

Assessment of Skills for Each Major (Communication Majors and Journalism Majors)

Freshman Year. *Freshman Information Literacy Seminar* (for both communication ma-jors and journalism majors): Students in the Freshman Information Literacy Seminar will prepare a library Web-based research inventory (Figure 6.6) for their assignments. The

INFORMATION NEED (for example, "Fact," "Statistic," "Biography," "Geographic location," "Definition" "Explanation," "Communication Theory")	SPECIFIC QUESTION (and date of assignment)	SOURCES REFERENCED	WHICH SOURCE WAS THE MOST EFFECTIVE FOR THIS QUESTION? (Identify with a check √)	WHICH INFORMATION LITERACY OBJECTIVE HAVE I LEARNED IN THIS PROCESS? (Note: Objective A, B, C, D, E, F or G)
	Date of assignment: Specific question:			

Figure 6.6 Research Inventory.

inventory will be maintained for all four years of the major. Librarians will have access to each research inventory and will review each student's inventory at least once/year. The inventories will be linked to the student's e-mail address and librarians will respond with additional recommendations or comments as necessary. Librarians will determine the skills that require the most emphasis and reinforcement based upon their aggregated review of the research inventories. Where possible, librarians will observe and review the students' speech presentations to ascertain the degree of research (with noted attributions) for the preparation of the speech.

Sophomore Year. No core courses are taught during this year when students select courses from their selected track. Professors in the Communication and Journalism Department teaching sophomore-level courses will determine the effectiveness of the students' research process based upon the resulting products (e.g., papers, speeches). Recommendations from these professors for reinforcement of specific information literacy skills will be provided to the librarians. Librarians will review the exercises completed by the students designed to emphasize the significance of Objective E (comparing/contrasting information, developed to the comprehension level during the sophomore year) and Objective F (judging the value of a resource, developed to the application level during the sophomore year). Librarians will also determine the skills that require the most emphasis and reinforcement based upon their aggregated review of the research inventories. Where possible, librarians will observe and review the students' speech presentations to ascertain the degree of research (with noted attributions) for the preparation of the speech.

Junior Year. Librarians will review the exercise designed to emphasize the significance of Objective E (comparing/contrasting information, developed to the application-analysis levels during the junior year) and Objective F (judging the value of a resource, developed to the analysis-synthesis levels during the junior year). Professors teaching the COM-301, Communication Law, and COM-302, Communication Ethics courses will provide the librarians with feedback regarding student use of government sources and with their determination of the students' success of learning Objectives E and F. Librarians will continue to have access to each research inventory and will review each student's inventory at least once/year. The inventories will be linked to the student's e-mail address and librarians will respond with additional recommendations or comments as necessary. Librarians will also determine the skills that require the most emphasis and reinforcement based upon their aggregated review of the research inventories.

Senior Year. Librarians will continue to have access to each research inventory and will review each student's inventory at least once/year. The inventories will be linked to the student's e-mail address and librarians will respond with additional recommendations or comments as necessary. The completed inventories will be reviewed by the librarians to determine the overall level of proficiency of learning the information literacy objectives. (This process may be completed with a random sample.) The communication and journalism professors will review the completed inventories and, together with input from librarians where necessary, include their assessment of the students' information literacy skill development in the final student grade for the Senior Seminar.

REFERENCES

Accrediting Council on Education in Journalism and Mass Communications (ACE-JMC). *Standards for Accreditation* (2004). http://www2.ku.edu/~acejmc/BREAKING/New_standards_9–03.pdf (accessed September 27, 2007).

Brown, Pamela A., and Yun Xia. *Assessment Report of the Communication and Journalism Department*. Lawrenceville, NJ: Rider University, 2007.

Griffin, Cindy L. *Invitation to Public Speaking* (2nd ed.). Belmont, CA: Thomson Wadsworth, 2006.

Hynd-Shanahan, Cynthia, Jodi Patrick Holschuh, and Betty P. Hubbard. "Thinking Like a Historian: College Students' Reading of Multiple Historical Documents." *Journal of Literacy Research* 36(2) (2004): 141–176.

Rider University. *Undergraduate Catalog 06/07*. Lawrenceville, NJ: Rider University, 2006.

Rouet, Jean-Francois, M. Anne Britt, Robert A. Mason, and Charles A. Perfetti. "Using Multiple Sources of Evidence to Reason about History." *Journal of Educational Psychology* 88(3) (1996): 478–493.

Schaus, Margaret. "Hands-On History." *College and Research Libraries News* 9 (1990): 825–831.

Yancheff, Catherine. "Information Competencies for the Journalism Professional." Arcata, CA: Humboldt State University Library. (Last updated October 10, 2005). http://library.humboldt.edu/~ccm/fingertips/journal1.html (accessed March 14, 2008).

7

Recommended Sequence for Bibliographic and Information Literacy: College of Business Administration, the Business Core and Non-Business Core Courses

Our College of Business Administration (CBA) is accredited by The Association to Advance Collegiate Schools of Business (AACSB). In alignment with the AACSB accreditation requirements, the curriculum is grounded in core courses, known as either the "business core" or the "non-business core." The courses begin during the freshman year and conclude with a capstone core course during the final semester of the senior year. Students simultaneously fulfill the requirements for their declared major during the junior and senior years.

We needed to determine the information literacy skill preparation needed by the conclusion of the sophomore year to prepare all students for embarking on the courses required for their major. We then needed to identify information literacy requirements for each major, while incorporating the skills taught in the core courses taken in the junior and senior years.

In order to ensure that we were succeeding in the skill development, we needed to assess the skills at the conclusion of the sophomore year core curriculum and again at the conclusion of the senior year within each major. This meant developing information literacy objectives for the majors of accounting, actuarial science, advertising, economics, business administration, computer information systems, entrepreneurial studies, finance, global business, human resource management, management and leadership, and marketing. Illustrations here are given for the learning objectives for the business core and non-core courses (assessed first at the sophomore level and again at the conclusion of each major), and learning objectives for economics (Chapter 8) and entrepreneurial studies (Chapter 9) (also assessed at the conclusion of the major).

JUSTIFICATION

The skill sequence is intended to reinforce cross-learning of information literacy skills and to avoid unnecessary duplication of the teaching of the skills. Justification for the skill sequence comes from many sources, including the university's strategic plan, the mission statement of our own CBA, the accreditation standards of AACSB, and the accreditation standards of our accrediting body, the Middle States Commission on Higher Education. The CBA mission statement notes that "business students participate in a learning environment that offers both the practical skills needed to launch a career and the learning skills needed for continued growth" (Rider University, 2006, 14); these skills include information literacy skills.

In their discussion of the "more general intellectual or cognitive competencies and skills, which . . . are . . . thought to be salient outcomes of postsecondary education," Pascarella and Terenzini note that "these cognitive skills go by a number of different names—critical thinking, reflective judgment, epistemological development, and so on—and they differ somewhat in conceptual definition and the types of problems or issues they address. They do, however, have as a common theme the notion of applicability and utility across a wide range of different content areas. These cognitive competencies and skills represent the general intellectual outcomes of postsecondary education that permit individuals to '*process and utilize new information*; communicate effectively; reason objectively and *draw objective conclusions from various types of data; evaluate new ideas and techniques efficiently; become more objective about beliefs, attitudes, and values; evaluate arguments and claims critically*; and *make reasonable decisions in the face of imperfect information*. These and related general cognitive skills are a particularly important resource for the individual in a society and world *where factual knowledge is becoming obsolete at an accelerated rate*'" (Pascarella and Terenzini, 1991, 114–115, as quoted in Pascarella and Terenzini, 2005, 155) (author's italics).

While information literacy provides the obvious foundation for the skills identified by Pascarella and Terenzini, the evaluation level of information literacy skill development is clearly defined in their discussion of critical thinking. "There are many different definitions of, and ways of measuring, critical thinking. However, it would appear that most attempts to define and measure critical thinking operationally focus on an individual's capability to do some or all of the following: identify central issues and assumptions in an argument, recognize important relationships, *make correct references from the data, deduce conclusions from information or data provided, interpret whether conclusions are warranted based on given data, evaluate evidence or authority*, make self-corrections, and solve problems. Typical in measurement of these dimensions of critical thinking is the notion that some answers or solutions are *more verifiably correct than others*" (Pascarella and Terenzini, 2005, 156) (author's italics).

Concern about the information literacy skill level of college graduates has existed for some time. "An early 1990s alumni survey of The National Center for Post Secondary Improvement (2001) reported that only 48 percent of respondents reported confidence in their ability to find information. Business information has its own idiosyncrasies that contribute to greater difficulty. Business publications originate from diffuse sources. Therefore, there is a greater need for comparing, verifying, and corroborating information using multiple sources" (Fiegen, Cherry, and Watson, 2002, 308).

Not only do students require technical computer skills, but, as noted above, they need the information literacy skills of locating and evaluating authoritative information. "To be successful in a constantly changing and competitive workplace, and with 'an increasing awareness that information has become the leading business asset,' business students must be information literate. 'Indeed, many business leaders have proclaimed that their business is not products or services, but information that is used creatively to build the products or services to satisfy customers. The concept of the *knowledge company* is becoming more than just an esoteric business term. The successful companies are those that can turn data (raw materials) into information (finished goods) and then into knowledge (meaningful action based on the information)'" (Kanter, as quoted in Cooney and Hiris, 2003, 215).

Cooney and Hiris (2005) note a comprehensive study by Hawes that reviewed information literacy in business schools. Hawes concluded that "today's business school graduate is not being adequately prepared to function in an information-literate fashion" and that not enough is being done" (Hawes, as quoted in Cooney and Hiris, 2003, 215).

Standards

The standards of the AACSB include several references to aspects of information literacy. Strategic Management Standard 5 includes the expectation for the provision of "library and other information access" (AACSB, 2006, 27) and the phrase "modern business is highly information dependent" (28). In the Assurance of Learning Standard 15, "faculty from non-business disciplines" (71) (i.e., librarians) are included in those responsible for input into curriculum management. Included also in this standard are the general knowledge and skill areas of "use of information technology" (71) and "reflective thinking skills" (71). Other standards supporting the need for information literacy, of course, include those of the Middle States Commission on Higher Education (2003) and those provided by the Association of College & Research Libraries (ACRL).

Best Practice

The California State University Information Competence Project has identified both core competencies and discipline area competencies specific to business (http://www.lib.calpoly.edu/infocomp/specific_bs.html). Topics include business plans/ entrepreneurship; company, industry and international information; and knowledge of regulatory information. Each of these was considered when developing our information literacy standards for our CBA curriculum.

INFORMATION LITERACY IN THE CBA CORE COURSES

The curriculum of the CBA was reviewed to ensure that all required course content would be supported by our information literacy objectives. The CBA foundational business and non-business core of courses is linked to the accreditation requirements of the AACSB. Students also complete a general education core and coursework required for their selected major, beginning in their junior year. Taken simultaneously with the core during the freshman year is a required Freshman Seminar for business majors, intended to be an informational program, which includes the "effective use of Rider's resources" (Rider University, 2006, 14). The core includes five areas, with each area supported by several courses.

Content included in Principles of Marketing (MKT-200), Introduction to Finance (FIN-300), and Production and Operations (MSD-340) courses provides a "background of the concepts, processes, and institutions in the production and marketing of goods

and/or services, and the financing of the business enterprises or other forms of organization" (Rider University, 2006, 15). Background information included in Principles
of Microeconomics (ECO-201) and the Social and Legal Environment of Business
(BUS-300) courses focuses on the "economic and legal environment as it pertains to
profit or nonprofit organizations, along with ethical considerations and social and political influences as they affect such organizations" (Rider University, 2006). A "basic
understanding of the concepts and applications of accounting, quantitative methods,
and management information systems, including computer applications" (Rider University, 2006) is covered in Introduction to Computing (CIS-185), Principles of Financial
Accounting (ACC-210), Principles of Managerial Accounting (ACC-220), Statistical
Methods I and II (MSD-200 and MSD-201), and Management Information Systems
(CIS-485). Courses in composition (CMP-120, Expository Writing, and CMP-125, Research Writing) and speech (COM-290, Professional and Strategic Speech) together with
Fundamentals of Management and Organizational Behavior (MGT-201) cover content
in the "study of organization theory, behavior and interpersonal communications" (Rider
University, 2006). The capstone course, Strategic Management and Policy (BUS-400)
covers the "study of administrative processes under conditions of uncertainty, including
integrating analysis and policy determination at the overall management level" (Rider
University, 2006). In order to develop a sequence, we needed to identify which courses
were required for each year for both the core and non-core courses. This provided us
with the ability to reinforce learning from one course to the next and from one year to
the next without duplication of efforts. Figure 7.1 provides such an outline.

YEAR TAKEN	SEMESTER TAKEN	COURSE NO.	COURSE TITLE	CORE: BUSINESS or NON-BUSINESS
Freshman	Fall		Freshman Seminar	NA/Required
Freshman	Either	MSD-105	Quantitative Methods for Business	Non-business
Freshman	Either	CIS-185	Introduction to Computing	Non-business
Freshman	Fall	CMP-120	Expository Writing	Non-business
Freshman	Spring	CMP-125 or CMP-203	Research Writing (or Literature and Composition)	Non-business
Sophomore	Fall	ACC-210	Introduction to Accounting	Business
Sophomore	Fall	MSD-200	Statistical Methods I	Non-business
Sophomore	Fall	ECO-200	Principles of Macroeconomics	Non-business
Sophomore	Spring	ACC-220	Managerial Uses of Accounting	Business
Sophomore	Spring	MKT-200	Marketing Principles	Business
Sophomore	Spring	MGT-201	Fundamentals of Management and Organizational Behavior	Business
Sophomore	Spring	ACC-220	Managerial Uses of Accounting	Business
Sophomore	Spring	MSD-201	Statistical Methods II	Non-business
Sophomore	Spring	ECO-201	Principles of Microeconomics	Non-business
Sophomore	Either	COM-290	Professional and Strategic Speech	Non-business
Junior	Either	FIN-300	Introduction to Finance	Business
Junior	Either	MSD-340	Production and Operations	Business
Junior	Either	BUS-300	Social and Legal Environment of Business	Business
Senior	Fall	CIS-485	Management and Information Systems	Business
Senior	Spring	BUS-400	Capstone course: Strategic Management and Policy	Business

Figure 7.1 Sequence of CBA Core Business and Non-Business Courses.

Designing, Teaching, and Assessing the CBA Bibliographic and Information Literacy Sequence

The process involved in developing information literacy skills includes student development of problem solving, analytical and decision-making abilities, each of which were frequently noted in the objectives of the course syllabi (the objectives in the CBA course syllabi are quite extensive as they provide evidence of teaching goals and objectives for the AACSB evaluators). The information literacy objectives took into account each of the standards and the best practice noted above in addition to the content taught in the business core courses.

During the freshman year, we recognized the need to establish the business information literacy sequence, although there were only a few opportunities for students to practice the skills with core course assignments. This was of concern to us since our library instruction program mission is based upon course-integrated instruction with multiple opportunities for the students to practice their skills.

It was decided to incorporate the information literacy sequence into the required Freshman Seminar, which meets for one hour each week in the fall and is required of all business majors. There are sixteen sections of the seminar, with two sections exclusive to accounting majors. We considered other possible teaching opportunities, including a nonrequired Introduction to Business course, which accommodates 40 percent of the freshmen, and business clubs dedicated to each major. Students in the Accounting Club had requested business source-specific instruction in the past and this may be an opportunity for some institutions although we decided against it since academic clubs are not a requirement and we were seeking a level of student commitment more likely to occur in a required course. We, thus, selected the seminar since we would be addressing all freshman business majors during their first semester.

We will incorporate exercises into our sessions that will provide the opportunity to practice the skills and we will also be able to reinforce the skills in the Introduction to Computing (CIS-185) course, which includes at least one assignment requiring research. The exercises will include practice with sources related to accounting, economics, marketing, and management, in order to provide an introduction to sources that will be utilized for the core courses in those disciplines. An additional opportunity for skills reinforcement exists in the required composition course, Research Writing.

The following objectives (see Figure 7.2) are introduced in the freshman year. Two of the objectives are graduated and intended to be developed to higher cognitive levels with each year of study. Successful completion of the Freshman Seminar will require that the students satisfactorily complete the information literacy exercises. Students will recognize that mastery of the skills will be expected of them in each core course, culminating in a successful assessment of their proficiency for their graduation requirement from the CBA program.

One of the freshman non-business core courses is the Research Writing course, which is assessed separately. There should be a diligent attempt to avoid duplicating the instruction in this composition course and to instead extend the skills by emphasizing information-seeking skills required of business students.

Several of the learning objectives for the freshman year involve familiarizing the students with the business literature and introducing evaluative techniques specific to the business environment. Since most of this introduction will take place in the Freshman Seminar and not be integrated into the core courses until the sophomore year, there need

Freshman Year

Objective A (Introduced in the Freshman Year): Students will understand knowledge production for the business professions, including the ability to distinguish between primary, secondary, and tertiary types of research. [Cognitive levels: comprehension and application] (*Relates to ACRL Standards 1 & 2*)

Objective B (Introduced in the Freshman Year): Students will identify and investigate authoritative business sources (both print and electronic) for furthering their knowledge about the functional areas of business (accounting, finance, marketing and/or advertising, operations, management, human resources management, and information technology) and their interrelationships. Students will identify and investigate sources for enhancing their understanding of current economic issues that affect business and society (domestic and international). These will include reference sources for background reading (e.g., encyclopedias, guides, dictionaries, biographical sources, bibliographies, handbooks and yearbooks (e.g., *Europa World Year Book*), book catalogs, company data, industry data, statistical sources (e.g., *Statistical Resources on the WEB*/University of Michigan), legal sources (local, state, and federal), regulatory information (local, state, and federal), currency data, census/demographics (e.g., economic census, county business patterns), international information (export/import, trade barriers, country information), subject indexes and abstracts of business journals (e.g., *ABI-Inform*), relevant disciplinary indexes and abstracts of scholarly and professional journals, relevant citation indexes, indexes to general (including popular) periodicals, indexes to newspapers, relevant business Web sites (e.g., *Yahoo! Finance*), and respected research organizations. [Graduated skill development throughout sequence from cognitive levels of comprehension to synthesis.] (*Relates to ACRL Standards 1 & 2*)

Objective C (Introduced in the Freshman Year): Students will recognize the difference between scholarly, professional, and trade journals and identify major business journals. [Cognitive level: comprehension] (*Relates to ACRL Standards 1 &2*)

Objective D (Introduced in the Freshman Year): Students will identify and utilize resources for the background and industry trends for typical career paths followed by individuals who major in a particular business area. [Cognitive level: application] (*Relates to ACRL Standards 1 & 2*)

Objective E (Introduced in the Freshman Year): Students will compile a working bibliography by identifying a variety of types and formats of potential sources of information that may include books, articles, and authoritative Web sites. [Cognitive level: application] (*Relates to ACRL Standards 1 & 2*)

Objective F (Introduced in the Freshman Year): Students will identify and document the potential usefulness of a source. [Graduated skill development throughout sequence from cognitive levels of application to analysis] (*Relates to ACRL Standard 3*)

Objective G (Introduced in the Freshman Year): Students will judge the value of a resource by noting its reliability, validity, accuracy, authority, timeliness, point of view or bias. [Graduated skill development throughout sequence from cognitive levels of knowledge to evaluation] (*Relates to ACRL Standard 3*)

Objective H (Introduced in the Freshman Year): Students will be able to compare/contrast and critically evaluate information from multiple sources in order to ensure the accuracy of the information used. [Graduated skill development throughout sequence from cognitive levels of application to evaluation] (*Relates to ACRL Standard 3*)

Objective I (Introduced in the Freshman Year): Students will understand economic, legal, and social issues surrounding the use of information and access and use information ethically and legally, including recognizing copyright laws. Students will appropriately acknowledge their sources, including appropriately acknowledging quotations, accurately quoting, paraphrasing, and avoiding plagiarism. [Cognitive level: application] (*Relates to ACRL Standard 5*)

(Objectives J, K, & L are introduced in the sophomore year and identified ahead.)

Figure 7.2 CBA Core Information Literacy Objectives.

to be a series of assignments developed to provide students with the opportunity for the skills to become a part of their repertoire. Knowledge of the following business sources will provide a solid base from which the students can then branch out during their sophomore year core courses. These sources are included in subject guides available on the library's Web page.

The content of the curriculum for the freshman information literacy development will include the following elements (see Figure 7.3).

Primary literature

Business Standards
Business Associations and Institutions
    Internship opportunities
    Career opportunities
Company Data
    Annual Reports
    Officers
    Financial Statements and Data
    Products and Operations
    History
    Competition
    Reports provided within database collections
    Investment services
Industry Data
    Current Industry Environment
    Profile
        Trends
        Operations
        Key Ratios and Statistics
Economic data
    Consumer Price Index (CPI)
    Producer Price Index (PPI)
Laws and Regulations—Domestic and International
    State(s) law
    Federal law
    Regulatory systems
    Legislatures
    Anti-trust regulation
    Trade restrictions and regulations
Exchange rate
International monetary system
Market Research
    Domestic
    Global
Marketing
    Domestic
        Consumer
        Product
    Global
Management
    Organizational behavior
        Private sector
        Public sector
        Individual behavior
        Interpersonal relations
        Cultural diversity
        Ethics
        Management Trends
        Effective Management Practices for the Global Environment
International Trade
Investment
    Domestic
    International

Figure 7.3 Freshman Year CBA Bibliographic Outline.

Secondary literature

Books
Textbooks
Peer-reviewed journal articles (scholarly) in relevant disciplinary databases covering the following disciplines:
    Technology
    Economics
    Management
    Marketing
Related professional literature covering the following key business topics:
    Social policies
    Corporate practices
    Effects of government and business response
    Technology
    Social change and trends
        Consumer protection
        Product liability
        Employment discrimination
    Business "values"
        Ethical considerations
        Profit making goals
        Competition
        Growth
Conference papers
Dissertations

Tertiary literature

Hybrid Tools:
Encyclopedias
Yearbooks
Histories

Fact Tools:
Statistical sources
Handbooks
Dictionaries
Directories
Almanacs
Biographical sets
Atlases
Gazetteers

Guides:
    Guides to reference books
    Guides to business literature

Finding Tools:
Subject Guides dedicated to business topics provided on the library's Web page
Bibliographies (citations, essays)
Subject Specific Indexes & Abstracts
    Controlled vocabulary
Relevant Interdisciplinary Indexes & Abstracts
Indexes & Abstracts of Newspaper articles
Catalogs
"Free" Web information seeking
    Search engines
    Business Web sites
    Invisible Web

Figure 7.3 (continued)

Assessment in the Freshman Year

Students will begin during their freshman year to develop a required portfolio, or self-selected collection of assignments and research logs, to demonstrate information literacy skills learned in the areas of marketing, management, finance, economics, and accounting. The portfolio will be maintained at the library's Web page for access by students, librarians, and business faculty, and will include assignments and resources used for business assignments. For examples of a research log and a research inventory, see Chapter 4, Figure 4.2 and Chapter 6, Figure 6.6. Development of the portfolio will begin as students utilize resources for the Freshman Seminar assignments (which will be graded as either "Satisfactory" or "Unsatisfactory"). The library liaisons to the CBA will review the portfolios, determine whether satisfactory skill levels have been attained, and make determinations for areas of skill development that need to be reinforced during the sophomore year.

Sophomore Year

This year presents multiple opportunities to reinforce the objectives taught in the freshman year while incorporating the objectives into course-integrated instruction within the core courses. The accounting courses include an information literacy component (e.g., using accounting codes and regulations) taught by the accounting professors, who include multiple assignments with which the reference librarians assist students. The opportunity exists to reinforce all of the freshman year objectives while developing Objectives A, B, and G to the application level. The core courses offering this opportunity are Principles of Macroeconomics, Marketing Principles, Fundamentals of Management and Organizational Behavior, Principles of Microeconomics, and Professional and Strategic Speech. Objective H will be developed to the analysis level.

In the Marketing Principles (MKT-200) course, students are required to locate government information, particularly regulatory information, hence the opportunity to introduce Objective J (see Figure 7.4). The speech course is open only to business majors and the speech topics require company and industry research, thus providing an appropriate opportunity to introduce Objective K (ahead). Objective L (ahead) will be introduced and reinforced in both economics courses.

Assessment in the Sophomore Year

An additional piece of data will be added to the portfolio during the sophomore year: the course name and specific assignment that the sources were used for. Library liaisons will observe and review a sampling of speeches in the COM-290, Professional and Strategic Speech, course to determine the level of success in information seeking for their company-related speeches.

Library liaisons to CBA will again review the portfolios and determine, based upon both the quality of information literacy skill development demonstrated in the speeches and in the portfolios, the teaching emphasis needed for information literacy skill development during the junior year core courses.

Junior Year

This year is an important year to both deepen the skills within the core courses while also introducing specific skills and resources for students beginning the coursework for

Objective J (Introduced in the Sophomore Year): Students will understand how government information is organized and identify the need to access information from authoritative municipal, state, federal, or international government sources, including utilizing transcripts of Senate hearings and publications from government agencies such as the Bureau of Labor Statistics and U.S. Census Bureau. [Graduated skill development throughout sequence from cognitive levels of knowledge to evaluation, attaining the application level during the sophomore year] (*Relates to ACRL Standards 1 &2*)

Objective K (Introduced in the Sophomore Year): Students will gather extensive data and background information of an organization (e.g., philosophy; mission; purpose; objectives; history; description; current operational environment; strategies employed: functional, business, corporate, global, and competitive-level; whether the organization has embraced the corporate citizenship philosophy; whether the organization has implemented any "citizenship initiatives"; federal regulatory agencies influencing business practices; recent litigation [if any]; product recall[s] [if any]; Internet practices; the role of individuals; motivational strategies [employees]; identification of a unionized workforce; labor disputes [if any]; ethics; marketing of products/services; performance analysis; internal and external environmental analysis). In addition, they will gather objective information about the industry structure and environment within which the organization operates (including developments, trends, projections, and financial ratios). They will use this information to forecast trends and strategic directions for the future of the selected organization(s). This process will require utilization of objective industry, corporate and organizational sources as well as relevant statistical sources, indexes, and abstracts. [Graduated skill development throughout sequence from cognitive levels of knowledge to evaluation, attaining the application level during the sophomore year] (*Relates to ACRL Standards 1 &2*)

Objective L (Introduced in the Sophomore Year): Students will identify and utilize the resources for further investigating the role of markets, trade among nations, factors influencing the economy in the long run (e.g., economic institutions, political systems, legal and regulatory environment, development and diffusion of technology), and factors influencing the economy in the short run (e.g., economic fluctuations, fiscal policy, monetary policy). [Graduated skill development throughout sequence from cognitive levels of knowledge to evaluation, attaining the application level during the sophomore year] (*Relates to ACRL Standards 1 &2*)

Figure 7.4 Objectives Introduced in the Sophomore year.

their major. All three business courses provide the opportunity to reinforce all of the skills and to develop the skills of Objectives B, F, G, J, K, and L to the analysis level and develop Objective H to the synthesis level.

Assessment in the Junior Year

In addition to continuing the portfolio review, library liaisons will review a sampling of papers submitted in the BUS-300, Social and Legal Environment of Business, to determine the level of information seeking and the resulting incorporation of information into the papers. (For example, see the review of papers in the sociology sequence, Chapter 10.)

Assessment method: Library liaisons will provide an illustration of a completed business research plan (made available on the library's Web page) (see Figure 8.3). Students who have completed the Business Core and Non-Core courses at the 200–300 level will be given a business research question prepared by library liaisons in collaboration/consultation with the CBA faculty (at the completion of the 300-level courses, in BUS-300, FIN-300 and MSD-340). Multiple research questions appropriate to the content and research expectations of the business core will be prepared so that there are no duplicates. The students will be given one week (take home) to prepare a research plan for the particular question. Librarians (liaisons to departments in CBA) will share in the process of determining whether the students' research plans are "Satisfactory" or "Unsatisfactory" and provide these grades to the professor, who will determine the final grade for this research plan (to be incorporated into their grade for BUS-300, FIN-300, or MSD-340). The results of the research plans will inform the librarians of improvements needed in the teaching of the business information literacy skills.

Senior Year

Both the CIS course and the capstone course provide skill reinforcement opportunities, with the capstone course providing the opportunity to focus on the interrelationship of the business and interdisciplinary resources. While Objective B will be developed to the synthesis level, and Objectives G and H will be developed to the evaluation level, the following objectives will be developed to the synthesis and evaluation levels during this year: Objectives J, K, and L. The bibliographic and information literacy skills of the students will be assessed twice during this year and for two different purposes, once within the capstone course to determine the successful integration of the skills within the business core and within their major to assess the specific skills needed to be successful in the information-seeking requirements of their chosen field of study.

Capstone Course

The capstone assignment in Strategic Management and Policy (BUS-400) provides the opportunity to incorporate an integration of the information literacy skills. The assignment requires using information-seeking skills to perform an external analysis of a company (identification of industry opportunities and threats), internal analysis of the company (distinctive qualities, competitive advantage, and profit factors), and strategic analysis and diagnosis that results in a strategic choice. In order to successfully complete this assignment, students must utilize the skills learned throughout the sequence to access and apply information related to their selected company in the areas of accounting, economics, finance, marketing, and management.

Assessment in the Senior Year

In addition to reviewing the students' portfolios (which will contribute to the final assessment), the library liaisons will review each project submitted in the BUS-400 course and either utilize a rubric (see Figure 10.5) or, again, assign a "Satisfactory" or "Unsatisfactory" assessment of the bibliographic and information skill level reached. (For larger institutions, a sample may be utilized. Some may also find that the use of a "Satisfactory/Unsatisfactory" assessment is a more efficient method than the use of a rubric.) Feedback will be provided to the professors teaching BUS-400 to be included in the final grade for the students in this course. As noted previously, this will be one portion of the assessment: the assessment of the skills developed within the core CBA curriculum. In addition, each major will be assessed according to specific information literacy skills required of the major. Examples follow in Chapter 8 and Chapter 9.

CONCLUSION

An overview of the CBA information literacy sequence and the assessment opportunities (see Figure 7.5) may be presented in table form, with an accompanying rubric, if desired, to be used for the capstone assessment of the core CBA information literacy sequence.

COURSE (**bold** designates **Business Core** courses required for majors in CBA; <u>underlined courses are Non-Business Core requirements</u>)	**COURSE DESCRIPTION** (*Source for descriptions*: Rider University. *Undergraduate Catalog 06/07.* Lawrenceville, NJ: Rider University, 2006.)	**SPECIFIC INFORMATION LITERACY SKILL(S) REQUIRED and COGNITIVE LEVEL OF INFORMATION LITERACY SKILL(S)**	**METHOD OF ASSESSMENT**
Freshman Seminar	*"Freshman seminar is a structured advising experience for new students enrolled in the CBA. Its purpose is to support students in making a smooth transition from high school to college by providing information and guidance in such areas as time management, study skills, and effective use of Rider's resources. Participation in freshman seminar is required for all freshmen."*	Objective A (Comprehension level) Objective B (Comprehension level) Objective C (Comprehension level) Objective D (Application level) Objective E (Application level) Objective F (Application level) Objective G (Comprehension level) Objective H (Application level) Objective I (Application level)	Library-developed exercises will earn a "Satisfactory" or "Unsatisfactory" grade. Portfolio will be assessed by librarians.
BUSINESS CORE: **ACC-210-** Introduction to Accounting (*Sophomore Level*)	Course Description: *"A conceptual introduction to basic accounting principles and financial statements. Consideration is given to accounting for merchandising concerns, current assets, long-term assets, liabilities, and equity accounts. A brief overview of internal control and selected complex accounting topics is also presented."*	Accounting Department information literacy sequence	Exercises developed by the Accounting professors determine success of learning the information literacy skills.
ACC-220- Managerial Uses of Accounting (*Sophomore Level*)	Course Description: *"An exploration of how accounting information can be used as a management tool. Examines cost behavior patterns, cost classifications, and the problem-solving functions of accounting as they pertain to planning, control, evaluation of performance, special decisions, and long-range planning. The interpretation and uses of published financial statements, cash flow, and the effects of inflation are also considered."*	Accounting Department information literacy sequence	Exercises developed by the Accounting professors determine success of learning the information literacy skills.
MKT-200- Marketing Principles (*Sophomore Level*)	Course Description: *"Market characteristics, consumer buying habits and motives, functions of marketing, and the fields of retailing and wholesaling—including the role of intermediates—are examined. Concepts and current practices in product development, pricing, promotion, distribution, and international marketing are studied."*	Reinforcement of: Objective A (developed to the Application level), Objective B (developed to the Application level), Objective C (Comprehension level), Objective D (Application level), Objective E (Application level), Objective F (Application level), Objective G (developed to the Application level), Objective H (developed to the Analysis level), Objective I (Application level), Introduced in this course: Objective J (Application level)	Portfolio will be assessed by librarians.

Figure 7.5 CBA Information Literacy Sequence and Assessment Opportunities.

MGT-201- Fundamentals of Management & Organizational Behavior (*Sophomore Level*)	*Course Description: "This course deals with the fundamentals of organizational behavior as they relate to management such as motivation, communications, and leadership. Behavior is examined at the individual, group, and organizational level. The management functions of planning, organizing, leading and controlling are addressed. The effects of global operations and the requirements of ethical behavior on managers are also explored."*	Reinforcement of: Objective A (developed to the Application level), Objective B (developed to the Application level), Objective C (Comprehension level), Objective D (Application level), Objective E (Application level), Objective F (Application level), Objective G (developed to the Application level), Objective H (developed to the Analysis level), Objective I (Application level)	Portfolio will be assessed by librarians.
FIN-300- Introduction to Finance (*Junior level*)	*Course Description: "An introduction to the environment, concepts, and techniques of financial management. Topics include forms of business organization, taxes, analysis of financial performance, financial planning, financial markets and interest rates, time value of money, bond and stock valuation, risk and return, capital budgeting, cost of capital, and international financial management."*	Reinforcement of: Objective A (Application level), Objective B (developed to the Analysis level), Objective C (Comprehension level), Objective D (Application level), Objective E (Application level), Objective F (developed to the Analysis level), Objective G (developed to the Analysis level), Objective H (developed to the Synthesis level), Objective I (Application level), Objective J (developed to the Analysis level), Objective K (developed to the Analysis level), Objective L (developed to the Analysis level)	Portfolio will be assessed by librarians. Research questions developed by librarians will require a Research Plan by the students (which will receive a "Satisfactory" or "Unsatisfactory" grade).
MSD-340- Production & Operations (*Junior Level*)	*Course Description: "This course introduces the concepts and techniques of designing and managing manufacturing and service systems and their operations effectively and efficiently. Major topics include product and process design, facility location, forecasting, aggregate planning, inventory management, material requirements planning, project management, just-in-time systems, quality assurance, linear programming, the transportation problem and queuing models. Current issues such as productivity, global competitiveness, and quality are also discussed."*	Reinforcement of: Objective A (Application level), Objective B (developed to the Analysis level), Objective C (Comprehension level), Objective D (Application level), Objective E (Application level), Objective F (developed to the Analysis level), Objective G (developed to the Analysis level), Objective H (developed to the Synthesis level), Objective I (Application level), Objective J (developed to the Analysis level), Objective K (developed to the Analysis level), Objective L (developed to the Analysis level)	Portfolio will be assessed by librarians. Research questions developed by librarians will require a Research Plan by the students (which will receive a "Satisfactory" or "Unsatisfactory" grade).
BUS-300-Social & Legal Environment of Business (*Junior Level*)	*Course Description: "The strategies by which organizations in the private as well as the public sectors interact with, adapt to, and attempt to influence their external environments are explored. The primary emphasis is on evaluating the effect of business and governmental decisions on the quality of life. The role of regulatory agencies and the impact of local and national legislation on organizational behavior are considered."*	Reinforcement of: Objective A (Application level), Objective B (developed to the Analysis level), Objective C (Comprehension level), Objective D (Application level), Objective E (Application level), Objective F (developed to the Analysis level), Objective G (developed to the Analysis level), Objective H (developed to the Synthesis level), Objective I (Application level), Objective J (developed to the Analysis level), Objective K (developed to the Analysis level), Objective L (developed to the Analysis level)	Sampling of papers will be assessed by librarians. Research questions developed by librarians will require a Research Plan by the students (which will receive a "Satisfactory" or "Unsatisfactory" grade).

Figure 7.5 (continued)

CIS-485- Management Information Systems (*Senior Level*)	*Course Description:* "*The course focuses on the use and management of information systems and technology for the strategic and operational advantage of the firm. Students learn the business value of information resources of a firm, which include a variety of hardware, software and communications technologies.*"	Reinforcement of: Objective A (Application level), Objective B (developed to the Synthesis level), Objective C (Comprehension level), Objective D (Application level), Objective E (Application level), Objective F (Analysis level), Objective G (developed to the Evaluation level), Objective H (developed to the Evaluation level), Objective I (Application level), Objective J (developed to the Synthesis & Evaluation levels), Objective K (developed to the Synthesis & Evaluation levels), Objective L (developed to the Synthesis & Evaluation levels)	Portfolio will be assessed by librarians.
BUS-400- Strategic Management and Policy (*Senior Level*) (*Capstone Course*)	*Course Description:* This course "*provides a framework for problem identification, analysis, and decision making within the organization. Students are given the opportunity to integrate and apply previously acquired knowledge of accounting, decision sciences, economics, finance, marketing, management, and statistics.*"	Reinforcement of: Objective A (Application level), Objective B (developed to the Synthesis level), Objective C (Comprehension level), Objective D (Application level), Objective E (Application level), Objective F (Analysis level), Objective G (developed to the Evaluation level), Objective H (developed to the Evaluation level), Objective I (Application level), Objective J (developed to the Synthesis & Evaluation levels), Objective K (developed to the Synthesis & Evaluation levels), Objective L (developed to the Synthesis & Evaluation levels)	Capstone assignment requires information literacy skills which will be assessed by librarians.
NON-BUSINESS CORE: <u>CIS-185-</u> Introduction to Computing (*Freshman level*)	*Course Description:* "*This course provides an introduction to the basic concepts of computer hardware, software, and communication systems. Additionally, students are introduced to the use of the campus network for communications and research via the Internet and World Wide Web.*"	Reinforcement (as possible) of: Objective A (Comprehension level), Objective B (Comprehension level), Objective C (Comprehension level), Objective D (Application level), Objective E (Application level), Objective F (Application level), Objective G (Comprehension level), Objective H (Application level), Objective I (Application level)	Portfolio will be assessed by librarians.
<u>CMP-120-</u> Expository Writing (*Freshman level*)	*Course Description:* "*Students will increase their competence in the critical reading of challenging college-level texts that engage significant ideas and in writing effective essays that advance a clear and meaningful thesis while demonstrating understanding of those texts.*"	Not applicable.	
<u>CMP-125-</u> Research Writing (*Freshman level*)	*Course Description:* "*Introduces students to the process of library research and documented writing. Emphasis will be on the refinement of critical reading, thinking, and writing strategies applied to multiple sources and documented papers.*"	Assessed separately (see Warner, in press)	

Figure 7.5 (continued)

COM-290- Professional & Strategic Speech (*Sophomore level*)	*Course Description:* "*Improves communication skills of business majors to compete successfully in the corporate world. Provides students with practical information necessary for effective communication in various business and professional settings. Covers communication processes, principles and models in the modern organization.*"	Introduced in this course: Objective K (Application level), Objective L (Application level)	Portfolio will be assessed by librarians.
ECO-200- Principles of Macroeco- nomics (*Sophomore level*)	*Course Description:* "*A collective view of income receiving and spending sectors of the national economy including households, businesses, and governments. Problems: What determines the level of output, income, and employment achieved by the economy? What determines the growth of national output and employment? National income accounting, income and employment theory, monetary system, general price level, business cycle, government policies designed to provide for full employment, price stability, and economic growth are covered. Prerequisite: MSD-104 or MTH-100S or passing grade on math placement exam.*"	Reinforcement of: Objective A (developed to the Application level), Objective B (developed to the Application level), Objective C (Comprehension level), Objective D (Application level), Objective E (Application level), Objective F (Application level), Objective G (developed to the Application level), Objective H (developed to the Analysis level), Objective I (Application level)	Portfolio will be assessed by librarians.
ECO-201- Principles of Microeconomics (*Sophomore level*)	*Course Description:* "*Market price systems are analyzed. The nature and characteristics of consumer and producer behavior, the theory of pricing in competitive and noncompetitive markets, and determination of the distribution of output are evaluated. Welfare, social control, monopoly, and income inequality are explored in the light of price theory. The role of the U.S. in the world economy is explored.*"	Reinforcement of: Objective A (developed to the Application level), Objective B (developed to the Application level), Objective C (Comprehension level), Objective D (Application level), Objective E (Application level), Objective F (Application level), Objective G (developed to the Application level), Objective H (developed to the Analysis level), Objective I (Application level)	Portfolio will be assessed by librarians.
MSD-105- Quantitative Methods for Business I (*Freshman level*)	*Course Description:* "*Systems of linear equations, matrix algebra, linear programming, basic probability theory, and selected applications of mathematics to finance are covered.*"	Not applicable.	
MSD-200- Statistical Methods I (*Sophomore level*)	*Course Description:* "*Methods and applications of descriptive and inferential statistics are examined. Topics include graphical techniques, descriptive measures, random variables, sampling distributions, and estimation and hypothesis testing for the mean of one population.*"	Not applicable.	
MSD-201- Statistical Methods II (*Sophomore level*)	*Course Description:* "*Topics include inference for proportions, comparison of two means, proportions and variances, simple linear regression, chi square tests, and the analysis of variance.*"	Not applicable.	

Figure 7.5 (continued)

REFERENCES

Association to Advance Collegiate Schools of Business (AACSB). *Eligibility Procedures and Accreditation Standards for Business Accreditation.* Tampa, FL: AACSB International, 2003, revised 2004, 2005, 2006. http://www.aacsb.edu/accreditation/business/STANDARDS.pdf (accessed February 2007).

Association of College & Research Libraries (ACRL). *Information Literacy Competency Standards for Higher Education* (2000). http://www.ala.org/ala/acrl/acrlstandards/informationliteracycompetency.cfm (accessed March 13, 2008).

California State University. The California State University Information Competence Project. *Competencies Specific to Business.* http:::://www.lib.calpoly.edu/infocomp/specific_bs.html (accessed September 29, 2006).

Cooney, Martha, and Lorene Hiris. "Integrating Information Literacy and its Assessment into a Graduate Business Course: A Collaborative Framework." *Research Strategies* 19(3/4) (2003): 213–232.

Fiegen, Ann M., Bennett Cherry, and Kathleen K. Watson. "Reflections on Collaboration: Learning Outcomes and Information Literacy Assessment in the Business Curriculum." *Reference Services Review* 30(4) (2002): 307–318.

Middle States Commission on Higher Education. *Developing Research & Communication Skills: Guidelines for Information Literacy in the Curriculum.* Philadelphia, PA: Middle States Commission on Higher Education, 2003.

Pascarella, E. T., and P. T. Terenzini. *How College affects Students: A Third Decade of Research* (vol. 2). San Francisco, CA: Jossey-Bass, 2005.

Rider University. *Undergraduate Catalog 06/07.* Lawrenceville, NJ: Rider University, 2006.

Warner, Dorothy. "Programmatic Assessment of Information Literacy Skills using Rubrics." *Journal on Excellence in College Teaching* (in press).

ADDITIONAL READINGS

D'Angelo, Barbara J. "Using Source Analysis to Promote Critical Thinking." *Research Strategies* 18 (2001): 303–309.

Karp, Rashelle S., ed. *The Basic Business Library: Core Resources* (4th ed.). Westport, CT: Greenwood Press, 2002.

Prince, William W., Marilyn M. Helms, and Paula L. Haynes. "Project-focused Library Instruction in Business Strategy Courses." *Journal of Education for Business* (January/February 1993): 179–183.

8

Recommended Sequence for Bibliographic and Information Literacy: Economics Major

In the earlier chapter, it was noted that students in the College of Business Administration (CBA) at our institution begin the coursework for their majors during their junior year, while continuing to complete coursework for the business core that culminates in a capstone course. Two different information literacy sequences need to be addressed: those for the business core and those for the major, in this case the economics major.

The process may begin with a review of the assessment goals for the major and a review of syllabi for the courses required for the major. In this case, two of the economics courses (ECO-200, Principles of Macroeconomics, and ECO-201, Principles of Microeconomics) are core courses taken during the sophomore year, providing a building block for the sequence. When providing library instruction for those two courses, librarians are encouraged to emphasize the sources introduced as foundational sources for those students continuing in the major.

A curriculum map will identify those courses where library instruction is currently being taught and those courses that provide a library instruction opportunity, based on the review of the course description and the course syllabi. A more elaborate curriculum map (see Figure 8.1) intended for librarian review would also include course objectives identified by the professors and details about the assignments.

YEAR TAKEN	SEMESTER TAKEN	COURSE NO.	COURSE DESCRIPTION (*Source for descriptions*: Rider University. *Undergraduate Catalog 06/07.* Lawrenceville, NJ: Rider University, 2006.)	LIBRARY INSTRUCTION (∗) or **Opportunity** (based on review of course description & syllabi)
Sophomore (Core course)	Fall	ECO-200: Principles of Macroeconomics	*Course Description: "A collective view of income receiving and spending sectors of the national economy including households, businesses, and governments. Problems: What determines the level of output, income, and employment achieved by the economy? What determines the growth of national output and employment? National income accounting, income and employment theory, monetary system, general price level, business cycle, government policies designed to provide for full employment, price stability, and economic growth are covered."*	Opportunity
Sophomore (Core course)	Spring	ECO-201: Principles of Microeconomics	*Course Description: "Market price systems are analyzed. The nature and characteristics of consumer and producer behavior, the theory of pricing in competitive and noncompetitive markets, and determination of the distribution of output are evaluated. Welfare, social control, monopoly, and income inequality are explored in the light of price theory. The role of the U.S. in the world economy is explored."*	Opportunity
Junior	Fall	ECO-210: Intermediate Macroeconomics	*Course Description: "An analytical study of modern aggregate economic theory. Emphasizes the measurement and determination of income, employment, and price levels, as well as economic policy in theory and practice."*	Opportunity
Junior	Spring	ECO-211: Intermediate Microeconomics	*Course Description: "This course is designed to give the student a thorough understanding of microeconomic theory. As such, the course will analyze the behavior of both consumers and producers, and how this behavior determines the price and quantity observed in the market. The course objective is to provide students with the necessary theoretical background to enable them to solve meaningful and practical problems. Thus, the course is both theoretical and applied in its orientation. The course will emphasize that economic theory can be used not only to solve market oriented problems, but social and public policy problems as well."*	Opportunity
Representative electives (6 required):				
Junior or Senior		ECO-300- Business Conditions Analysis & Forecasting	*Course Description: "Business conditions change daily. Students study them as they change, learning to understand them in the light of economic theory, learning how each part of the economy is affected, and learning the advantages and limitations of the most reliable forecasting methods."*	Opportunity

Figure 8.1 Curriculum Map for Economics Majors.

Junior or Senior	ECO-305- International Trade and Investment	Course Description: "Studies the theory, institutions, and structures underlying the international flow of trade and investment. Topics are: the theory of international trade; balance of payment analysis; the international monetary system; adjustment to balance of payment disequilibrium; regional economic integration; the economic effects of trade restrictions; and trade and foreign investment problems of developing nations."	Opportunity
Junior or Senior	ECO-315- Comparative Economic Systems	Course Description: "Provides a conceptual framework for classifying and comparing economic systems. Presents theory of the capitalist market economy and case studies of the U.S., Japanese, French, and Swedish economies. Examines theory of the centrally planned economy, its transition, and case studies of the Soviet and its successor states, Chinese, and East European economies. Case studies are necessarily limited, concentrating on selected topics, such as transition strategies, industrial policy, etc."	Opportunity
Junior or Senior	ECO-325- Industrial Organization	Course Description: "Explores the relationship between market structure and performance. Topics include concentration in individual industries, product differentiation and entry barriers, pricing and marketing policies, and antitrust policies and their consequences."	*
Junior or Senior	ECO-335- Economics of the Public Sector	Course Description: "Analyzes the economic roles of government: allocation; distribution; and stabilization. The course examines the tools used by governments, especially the federal government, such as taxation, expenditures, regulations and laws in order to achieve economic goals. The course will give special attention to social regulation."	*
Junior or Senior	ECO-336- Economics of the Health Care Sector	Course Description: "This course presents ways in which economic analysis can be used to explain issues in the health care industry. Microeconomic tools will be used to describe the behavior of consumers, producers, and third parties of the health care sector. The course also investigates the role of government in regulating the health care sector, and in providing services to the poor and elderly. Finally, we will use this foundation to examine some recent changes in this industry, and to analyze the most recent proposals for further changes."	*
Junior or Senior	ECO-360- Contemporary Economic Issues	Course Description: "Selected current issues are examined within the framework of economic theory."	Opportunity
Junior or Senior	ECO-365-The Post-Soviet Economy & U.S. Business	Course Description: "Studies the contemporary post-Soviet economic system with emphasis on institutions, policies and issues related to business opportunities in this area. Topics covered include the historic, geographic, political, and cultural setting, planning and plan implementation in the traditional system, current reforms and prospects for the future, with special reference to the foreign trade institutions and experience of foreign firms doing business in the post-Soviet Union and East European countries."	*
Senior	ECO-450- Seminar in Economic Research	Course Description: "Students in the course learn to conduct economic research by engaging in an actual community-based research project. At the beginning of the semester, students are assigned to a community-based organization. As a team, students meet with the client, devise a plan of action, collect and analyze data and other information, and write a report to the client. At the end of the semester, students present their findings to the client."	*

Figure 8.1 (continued)

ECONOMICS INFORMATION LITERACY OBJECTIVES LINKED TO THE ASSESSMENT GOALS

Assessment Goals for Economics

The assessment goals of the department are that "economics majors should be able to evaluate the *efficiency* and *distributional* consequences of decisions affecting resource use. They should also be able to communicate effectively the results of their evaluations to stakeholders and other interested parties, including those who lack formal training in economics" (Bentley, 2006, reprinted with permission from Rider University). Information literacy objectives were developed to support these goals which are information-dependent.

Information Literacy Objectives for Economics and the Content Required for a Curriculum Outline for Economics

In addition to the two CBA core introductory macroeconomics and microeconomics courses, there are two required courses for all economics majors, ECO-210: Intermediate Macroeconomics, and ECO-211: Intermediate Microeconomics. The economics information literacy objectives will be grounded in these four required courses.

The information literacy objective for macroeconomics will be for the students to identify, utilize, and evaluate both qualitative and quantitative sources that provide information about the "income receiving and spending sectors of the national economy including households, businesses, and governments" (ECO-200) and the practice of "measurement and determination of income, employment, price levels, as well as economic policy in theory and practice" (ECO-210) (Rider University, 2006). Specifics related to this macroeconomics information literacy objective are outlined ahead in the Assessment section of this chapter.

The information literacy objective for microeconomics will be for the students to identify, utilize, and evaluate both qualitative and quantitative sources that provide information on the "nature and characteristics of consumer and producer behavior, the theory of pricing in competitive and noncompetitive markets, and determination of the distribution of output" (ECO-201) and for analyzing how the behavior of both consumers and producers "determines the price and quantity observed in the market" (ECO-211) (Rider University, 2006). Specifics related to this microeconomics information literacy objective are outlined ahead in the Assessment section of this chapter.

The remaining course requirements for the economics major may be selected from electives which each take a specific economic focus, as, for example, the public sector, the health care sector, or the post-Soviet economy. For each of these courses, more specific objectives will be required, of course, in order to provide an informed background of topic-specific sources.

But in each case, students would be building upon the CBA core information literacy objective B and deepening their awareness of relevant economics sources. The tie, then, to the CBA core objectives would be a constant throughout this major, with increasing emphasis on relevant economics sources specific to each course focus. At some point in their study within the 300- and 400-level courses, it is expected that students will be exposed to the following sources (as shown in Figure 8.2).

Figure 8.2 Bibliographic Outline for Economics.

Handbooks

Economic Indicators Handbook: Time Series, Conversions, Documentation
Economist's Handbook
Handbook of U.S. Labor Statistics

Histories

Oxford Encyclopedia of Economic History

Associations

American Economic Association (http://www.aeaweb.org)
Econometric Society (http://www.econometricsociety.org)
European Economic Association (http://www.eeassoc.org)
National Association for Business Economics (http://www.nabe. com)

Figure 8.2 (continued)

Assessment of Economics Bibliographic and Information Literacy Skills in the Senior Level Seminar in Economic Research

The Assignment. The project in the seminar will be to select an issue for which an economic analysis can be provided. The issue must be data-based and the data must be available in a time series. The issue must then be placed within its appropriate context and further analyzed. For example, if the issue is "baseball," the student must examine the issue from the social and legal positions in addition to the economic position. If the issue is "shipping," then the legal aspects of maritime law could be considered.

Bibliographic Instruction. Students will be introduced to an example of a research process for an appropriate economics issue (although the example will be for instructional purposes only and the students will not be allowed to select it for their seminar project). They will be expected to demonstrate a similar research process for the issue that they select, and they are expected to appropriately apply the information literacy skills that they have learned in the 200- and 300-level courses to their project.

The instruction for the seminar will reinforce the importance of selecting the appropriate periodical index for the issue. Selections in the instructional example will include the *Journal of Economic Literature*, a political science database (e. g., *PAIS*), and a social sciences database (e. g., *Social Sciences Full Text*). The *Journal of Economic Literature* provides summaries of economic literature on a given topic, in addition to providing an index to economic literature (the portion included in the database, *EconLit*). Such summaries, or reviews of topics identified in *Economic Review*, can provide a valuable outline for the student's project. The assessment will include whether either of these review sources was appropriately utilized.

Identification of Relevant Sources. The students in the Seminar in Economic Research (ECO-450) will develop a preliminary research plan (Figure 8.3) for their project. Students will be informed that the grade for their term projects will include an assessment of their proficiency of economic information literacy. At least twice/semester, students will consult with the librarians (a requirement), who will make recommendations for additional resources. The completed term project will include a final research plan listing all of the sources consulted. In addition, for at least five of the sources consulted, students will provide an evaluation of the value of the source in comparison/contrast with the other sources used. Students will be guided in their source evaluation with specific questions prepared collaboratively by the librarians and economics faculty (Figure 8.3).

1. State your research problem.
2. List keywords that are identified with this problem.
3. Describe the type(s) of information and potential sources needed to complete the research (include multiple formats, e.g., books, articles, newspapers, free Web sites; include multiple information types as appropriate, i.e., company-specific sources, industry-specific sources, regulatory sources, legal information, statistical sources).

For example:

RESEARCH PLAN

1. State your research problem.

2. List keywords that are identified with this problem.

3. Describe the type(s) of information and potential sources needed (<u>below</u>) to complete the research (include multiple formats, e.g., books, articles, newspapers, free Web sites; include multiple information types, as appropriate, i.e., company-specific sources, industry-specific sources, regulatory sources, legal information, statistical sources).

INFORMATION NEEDED	POTENTIAL SOURCE(S) or TYPE OF RESOURCE	SOURCE(S) CONSULTED	INFORMATION NEED MET [√ = check]	CONSULT FURTHER WITH A LIBRARIAN (yes or no)
Labor statistics	Bureau of Labor Statistics (see BLS Web site and print statistical compilations in the reference area of the library)			
Company information	Company Web site(s) *Standard and Poor's* Business databases			
Local legal and regulatory information (labor-related)	State labor laws and regulations			
Articles in current business journals related to economics	*ABI-Inform* *EconLit* *Factiva*			

4. In preparation for accessing information in the databases, construct several possible search statements incorporating the skills learned in Research Writing (CMP-125) and reinforced in the upper-level courses (e.g., Boolean logic, truncation, nesting, controlled vocabulary). Refer back to your research problem and keywords for the vocabulary to use in your search statements.
5. Identify all sources consulted.
6. For at least five of the sources consulted, include an evaluation of the source. Describe how each source compares/contrasts in value with the other sources you have identified. Use this criteria to evaluate your sources:
   a. How did you know that the source and its content are reliable or trustworthy?
   b. How did you know that the source content is a valid or reputable study?
   c. How did you determine the author(s)' credentials and the authority for the information?
   d. How did you know that the information in the source is the most current or "timely"?
   e. How did you determine the likelihood of bias?
   f. How did you know that the information is accurate?
7. Describe advantages and disadvantages of searching the "free" World Wide Web versus utilizing subscription databases for the research for your particular project.

Figure 8.3 Research Plan.

The Macroeconomic Perspective

What is the effect of the national economy?
    The economy in the short run (economic fluctuations, fiscal policy, and monetary policy)
    The economy in the long run
    Receiving sector (income)
    Spending sector (output)
    Public sector
    Private sector
    Households
    Businesses (including the business cycle and fluctuations)
    Political Systems
        Governments (including policies)
    Employment and unemployment rates
    National income accounting
    Price stability and instability
    Monetary system
    Price indexes
    General price level determination
    Role of markets
    Economic institutions
    Legal and regulatory environment
    Development of technology
What is the effect of the global economy?
    Relationship to the U.S. economy
    Trade among nations

The Microeconomic Perspective

Consumer and producer behavior (and its effect on price and quantity observed in the market)
Pricing in competitive and noncompetitive markets
Determination of the distribution of output
Cost and production
    Alternative costs
    Interest
    Profits
Elasticity
Utility
Monopoly (private and regulated)
Scarcity
Income distribution
    Income inequality
    Wages
        Minimum wage laws
Social policy and legislation
    Welfare
Public policy
Labor unions
Rents

Figure 8.4 Checklist of Concepts related to Macroeconomics and Microeconomics to be addressed in the Student Senior Projects.

<u>Research Plan Illustration</u> (Figure 8.3 adapted from SSM 304 Project Planning Work-sheet, Fiegen, Cherry, and Watson, 2002, 317–318). This may be adapted for use at both the end of the business core (or at the end of the sophomore/beginning of the junior year before proceeding on to the courses for the major) and again at the conclusion of the student's major (senior year).

Assessment Queries. Each project will need to be assessed according to the selected issue. A checklist (Figure 8.4) of macroeconomic and microeconomic concepts will be reviewed for each project, recognizing that not all concepts will be relevant for every issue. What needs to be considered is whether the student has "thought through" the project as an economist would from both the macroeconomic and the microeconomic perspectives. This assessment needs to have input from both the economics faculty and from the librarians, both of whom will identify the collective strengths and weaknesses of the students' research processes in order to improve on their bibliographic and research process emphasis in future instructional sessions. The assessment will include the depth of source selection and analysis defined by the research plan and address how thoroughly the students organized and evaluated their information according to the checklist of concepts (those relevant to the student's project).

REFERENCES

Bentley, Jerry. *Assessment Report of the Economics Department*. Lawrenceville, NJ: Rider University, 2006.

Fiegen, Ann M., Bennett Cherry, and Kathleen K. Watson. "Reflections on Collaboration: Learning Outcomes and Information Literacy Assessment in the Business Curriculum." *Reference Services Review* 30(4) (2002): 307–318.

Rider University. *Undergraduate Catalog 06/07*. Lawrenceville, NJ: Rider University, 2006.

9

Recommended Sequence for Bibliographic and Information Literacy: Entrepreneurial Studies

Students selecting this major expect to manage their own business, join a family business, or work for a small company. Information literacy is integral to the success of students in this major area of study. During their junior year in Small Business Management (MGT-348), students prepare a preliminary plan for a small business that requires determining the market potential for their selected business. This requires conducting a thorough overview of the industry within which their business falls and a scrutiny of the demographics of the area where they plan to build their business. During the senior year, students prepare a much more extended plan, which begins with the determination of the market potential for the small business and also requires them to apply skills learned in the business core courses of accounting, marketing, and management. The application of these skills results in determining the scale of the operation, its layout and staffing, the type of financing, an estimation of the revenues and profits, and the presentation of an income statement, balance sheet, and cash flow projections. To reinforce the concepts learned in these core courses, professors from the accounting, marketing and management departments are invited to speak to the students in their chosen senior course (either MGT-448, Seminar in Small Business Consulting, or BUS-410, New Venture Planning) as they prepare for their final projects in their senior year.

Librarians are involved with students at both levels. Following an introductory session in MGT-348, MGT-448 or BUS-410, students return to the library as a group for two working sessions. They also contact the librarian(s) dedicated to the courses by e-mail and phone. The professors teaching in the program are also in close contact with the librarian(s) and inform them throughout the semester of student needs and gaps in the information trail.

The students' projects cannot be successful if the research has not been conducted appropriately. At the conclusion of the semester, there is feedback from the professors about the success of the projects, and recommendations are provided to the librarian(s) for improvements. In these ways, assessment is naturally built in. Librarians are continually recognizing the learning problems during the working sessions and following through with the students as professors assess the level of research at various stages in the semester. This is truly a shared responsibility for both the teaching and assessing of skills.

The curriculum for this major encompasses the following courses in Figure 9.1.

ASSESSMENT GOALS AND OBJECTIVES OF THE ENTREPRENEURIAL STUDIES MAJOR

Since the goals and objectives identified by the major include information literacy goals and objectives, it was not necessary for the library to develop them. Each of the following goals and objectives of the entrepreneurial studies program are information-dependent: "a) develop and apply secondary research skills to investigate a market for a new venture; b) develop a promotion plan, pricing strategy, and sales forecast for a new venture, with all decisions justified; c) develop a management plan for a new venture; d) develop an operation analysis for a new venture, with all personnel and non-personnel costs documented; e) using the data from 'a–d', develop a proforma cash flow statement, income statement, and balance sheet for three years for a new venture; f) using the above information, develop a written conclusion to the business plan that will recommend if the new venture idea is an opportunity or not; g) regardless of the decision in 'f', determine how the new venture concept as developed through the business plan could be improved" (Cook, 2007, reprinted with permission from Rider University).

BIBLIOGRAPHIC OUTLINE FOR MGT-348-SMALL BUSINESS MANAGEMENT

For the preliminary small business plan, the students must research the industry environment and the demographics of the area where they wish to place their business. Each small business plan requires sources beyond those below which cannot be anticipated until the student suggests a small business. Business-specific and association Web sites (e.g., restaurant.org) are identified as students identify questions and pursue the required information. Evidence must exist that the following research path (see Figure 9.2) has been taken and that the associated resources have been utilized effectively and documented properly in the plan.

BIBLIOGRAPHIC OUTLINE FOR BUS-410-NEW VENTURE PLANNING

In addition to researching the industry environment and the demographics of the area in which they plan to place their new venture, students must utilize sources in order to adequately describe the scale of the operation, its layout and staffing, the type of financing, an estimation of the revenues and profits, and the presentation of an income statement, balance sheet, and cash flow projections. The choice of the venture determines the level of creativity required for the research process. For the more complex plan, there must at least be evidence that the following sources (see Figure 9.3), in addition, to those noted in Figure 9.2, have been utilized.

LEVEL	COURSE NAME (required courses in bold)	COURSE DESCRIPTION (*Source for descriptions:* Rider University. *Undergraduate Catalog 06/07.* Lawrenceville, NJ: Rider University, 2006.)	ASSESSMENT OF INFORMATION LITERACY SKILLS
Junior	**MGT-348-Small Business Management**	*Course Description:* "The role of small business in the American economy is examined. Favorable practices, policies, functions, principles, and procedures of and for the small business entrepreneur and owner-manager are studied. Includes learning a method to evaluate a new venture idea."	*Assessment method*: Information literacy skills utilized for the preliminary small business plan are assessed by the business professor who provides immediate feedback to the librarian. Teaching improvements for information literacy skills are then developed for the next semester in which the course is taught.
Junior	**ACC-335-Small Business Taxation**	*Course Description:* "This course provides an understanding of the key tax issues faced by small businesses and their business implications. It also familiarizes prospective business owners with various tax filing requirements so that they can use the expertise of tax professionals more effectively."	
Junior or Senior	*3 of the following*: FIN-350-Entrepreneurial Finance	*Course Description:* "This course covers the techniques for acquiring financial resources as a firm advances through successive business stages: seed, start-up, struggling, growing, and stable. In addition, it examines recent trends in credit markets and the latest financial innovations as these impact the process of financing the venture's growth."	
Junior or Senior	MKT-350-Retailing Management	*Course Description:* "The principles underlying successful retailing are analyzed within the framework of the strategic-planning process. Topics covered include location, merchandise planning, customer service, image, atmosphere, layout, pricing, promotion, personnel and operations management."	
Junior or Senior	CBA-350-Family Business Management	*Course Description:* "This course is directed at understanding the family-owned and managed firm. Topics included are the strengths and weaknesses of a family firm, the dynamics of the family and business interactions, conflict resolution, succession planning, and ownership transfer. The course will help individuals involved with a family firm, regardless if they are a family member. Prerequisite: MGT-201."*	
Junior or Senior	BUS-214-Advanced Business Law	*Course Description:* "This course provides students with an introduction to the fundamentals of individual and organizational forms of doing business. The laws governing agency, partnerships, corporations, and the purchase and sale of securities will be explored. The legal consequences of the relationships, and the rights and duties of the parties and entities will be discussed, as will the rules of law governing real, personal, and intellectual property, including the transfer of title to real property, the various types of bailments, the landlord-tenant relationship, and the laws concerning wills, trusts, and estates. The concerns of businesses that compete in the global environment through the study of international law will also be discussed."	

Figure 9.1 Curriculum for the Entrepreneurial Studies Major (and Assessment of Information Literacy).

Junior or Senior	CIS-340-Electronic Commerce	*Course Description:* "Students will learn about the broad range of Internet business technologies; develop the skills necessary to create and administer successful electronic commerce projects; and understand the associated benefits, and risks of electronic commerce business models. Prerequisite: CIS-185."	
Junior or Senior	CBA-220-Minding Our Business	*Course Description:* "A community service mentoring project designed to promote leadership, teamwork and entrepreneurship among Trenton youth through a school-based team mentoring model. Students will undergo intensive training in leadership skills, communication skills, team building skills, cultural diversity, small business entrepreneurship, and problems of early adolescent development prior to their fieldwork experience. Students will form teams to mentor groups of students at a Trenton middle school in the creation and management of their own microbusinesses. Student journals, quizzes, field trips, and class meetings will serve to organize and structure experiential learning."	
Junior or Senior	MGT-310-Introduction to Human Resource Management	*Course Description:* "This course deals with the nature of human resource management, its functions, procedures, and practices currently found in profit, nonprofit, and public sector organizations. Topics covered include recruiting and selection, training, human resource development, equal employment opportunity, performance appraisal, diversity, job analysis, compensation, and employee rights and discipline."	
Junior or Senior	MGT-363-Management Skills	*Course Description:* "The focus of this course is on specific skills necessary for success in a management role. These skills include leading, communicating effectively, delegating, conflict and time management, and motivating others. Students will have opportunities to practice skills and to apply their knowledge to business cases. Prerequisite: MGT-201."	
	One of the following integrative experiential courses:		
Senior	**MGT-448-Seminar in Small Business Consulting**	*Course Description:* "This course utilizes student teams to assist existing small businesses in solving problems or researching opportunities. Students will spend the majority of time in the field utilizing an experiential learning approach. Weekly activity logs, proposal development, and project completion are required."	*Assessment method*: Information literacy skills utilized for the complex small business plan are assessed by the business professor who provides immediate feedback to the librarian. Teaching improvements for information literacy skills are then developed for the next semester in which the course is taught.
Senior	**BUS-410-New Venture Planning**	*Course Description:* "This course will require students to select a business and prepare a complete new venture plan for it. This plan would identify the product and its target market, analyze its market potential, choose the location, scale of operation, layout, staffing type of financing, estimate the revenues and profits, and present the income statement, balance sheet, and the cash flow projects."	*Assessment method*: Information literacy skills utilized for the complex small business plan are assessed by the business professor who provides immediate feedback to the librarian. Teaching improvements for information literacy skills are then developed for the next semester in which the course is taught.

Figure 9.1 (continued)

Identify the Industry
North American Industry Classification System (NAICS) http://www.census.gov/epcd/naics02

Seek General Industry Information
Business and Company Resource Center (database)
Standard and Poor's Net Advantage (database)
Small Business Sourcebook: The Entrepreneur's Resource

Locate Articles in Business Periodicals
ABI-Inform
Business Source Premier
Factiva
Wilson Business Full Text
Predicasts F & S Index

Identify Trade Organizations, Publications, and Trade Shows
Associations on the Net (http://www.ipl.org/div/aon)
Encyclopedia of Associations

Competition
Reference USA (database)
Market Share Reporter: An Annual Compilation of Reported Market Share Data on Companies

Commerce and Tourism
[State] Commerce Department (e.g., *NJ Commerce*: Business Prosperity for the New Century http://newjerseycommerce.org)
[State] Business Periodicals (e.g., *New Jersey Business*, *New Jersey Economic Indicators*, *Employment & the Economy* [in New Jersey])

Learning about the Consumers including Demographics and Geographics

Demographics:
Census State Data Centers (http://www.census.gov/sdc/www)
Municipal Databook(s) (e.g., *New Jersey Municipal Databook*)

Economics: (Including Consumer Expenditures, Payroll, & Number of Business Establishments)
Census Bureau Economic Programs (*County Business Patterns* and *Economic Census*) (http://www.census.gov/econ/www)
Monthly Retail Trade and Food Services (http://www.census.gov/mrts/www/mrts.html)
Consumer Expenditure Survey (http://stats.bls.gov/cex/home.htm)

Figure 9.2 Bibliographic Outline (Small Business Management).

Legal Information/Regulations
[State] Administrative Code
Business.gov (The Official Business Link to the U.S. Government) (http://www.business.gov)
Small Business Laws & Regulations (http://www.sba.gov)

Financial and Operating Ratios to Help Commercial Bankers Make Better Lending Decisions
Almanac of Business and Industrial Financial Ratios (Leo Troy)
RMA Annual Statement Studies (Risk Management Association)
Industry Norms and Key Business Ratios

Small Business Sources
Small Business Desk Reference
Encyclopedia of Small Business
U.S. Small Business Administration (http://www.sba.gov)

Government Information
USA.gov (http://www.usa.gov)
Google/U.S. Government Search (http://www.google.com/ig/usgov)
[State] Web site (e.g., *The Official State of New Jersey Web site* includes a business link for information about starting a business, operating a business, licensing & permitting, and more)
OSHA (*U.S. Department of Labor, Occupational Safety & Health Administration*) (http://www.osha.gov)
Internal Revenue Service, Tax Information for Businesses (http://www.irs.gov/businesses)

Linking Sites for More Sources
CEOExpress (http://www.ceoexpress.com)
Small Business Information (http://sbinformation.about.com)
Michigan eLibrary (See MeL Pathfinder: Business, Economics and Labor) (http://web.mel.org)
Entrepreneur.com (http://www.entrepreneurmag.com)

Figure 9.3 Bibliographic Outline (New Venture Planning).

REFERENCES

Cook, Ronald. *Assessment Report of the Entrepreneurial Studies Program.* Lawrenceville, NJ: Rider University, 2007.
Rider University. *Undergraduate Catalog 06/07.* Lawrenceville, NJ: Rider University, 2006.

10

An Example "In Process"—
Recommended Sequence for
Bibliographic and Information Literacy:
Sociology

The Sociology Department was approached for our first venture into disciplinary assessment because of the collegial working relationship that has been fostered by several librarians with the faculty in the department over many years. Within a typical sociology curriculum, information literacy will likely be addressed in an introductory course or introductory seminar intended for its majors (either a 100- or 200-level course). Intermediate-level and upper-level courses (300- or 400-level course) will require specific information literacy skills that will depend upon the type of sociology paper to be written (i.e., a social issue paper, critical evaluation of sociological literature, quantitative research paper, or qualitative research paper). The culminating capstone course or senior seminar (400-level) will provide the opportunity for programmatic assessment of the student learning outcomes for the sociology information literacy objectives. Library support will be required for each level and the collaborative working arrangement with the sociology faculty will determine the precise role for the librarians.

Two reference sources were identified and consulted for the development of the information literacy objectives: *The Sociology Student Writer's Manual* (the text used in the introductory seminar) and *Sociology: A Guide to Reference and Information Sources*. *The Sociology Student Writer's Manual* provides extensive information about conducting research in sociology, provides a research schedule that reinforces the process being introduced, and provides an example to build upon for assessing the attainment of information literacy skills. In addition to describing the process for doing social research, the manual identifies and describes guides to sociological literature (finding aids and content reference works), general periodicals and newspapers, academic journals (identifying the major journals in the field), methods for researching books, and specific U.S. government publications typically used by sociologists. To complement the research schedule, a research plan will be employed to include the following elements: stating the information need (e.g., statistics, background information, specific interdisciplinary information, fact check), the specific sources consulted, and the notation of the source(s) that best fill the information need (for an example, see the Research Inventory, Figure 6.6).

This proposal recommends focusing library support on the introductory and senior seminars. Where opportunities exist in the curriculum for students to practice their skills in the intermediate-level courses, library instruction should be provided as needed in order to reinforce the development of the skills learned in the introductory-level course and to further prepare the students for the capstone course. Due especially to the interdisciplinarity of sociology, information literacy for sociology majors is particularly complex, leading students to disciplines that include law, gender, race, urban sociology, and issues of population and demography.

DEVELOPING THE SOCIOLOGY INFORMATION LITERACY SEQUENCE

Reviewing Assessment Goals for Sociology Majors

The following model assessment goals (Truchil, 2006, reprinted with permission from Rider University) for sociology majors (see Figure 10.1) include many opportunities for curricular support with information literacy skills (see especially those in **bold**).

(1) Developing a "Sociological Imagination," defined as understanding and being able to do the following:
    a. Explain how society (structural, cultural, and group factors) influence personal interactions and relationships, and the development of the self.
    b. Explain how social interaction can also influence the larger social structure and culture of society.
(2) **Understanding how to collect and analyze sociological evidence/data, defined as the following:**
    a. Understand the range of sociological methods to gather data.
    b. Understand which methods are appropriate to specific questions and areas of inquiry.
    c. Understand how to read statistics, tables, graphs, to describe and summarize data, and to determine if it supports conclusions.
    d. Understand how to use data in a logical argument to support conclusions.
(3) **Analyzing and applying sociological literature, defined as the following:**
    a. Understand social concepts and theories.
    b. Summarize and explain literature in sociology.
    c. Analyze and critique arguments in the sociology literature.
    d. Apply relevant concepts to information and observations.
(4) **Preparing presentations of data, argument, and conclusions, defined as the following:**
    a. Communicate ideas effectively in oral and written forms.
    b. Organize papers and presentations logically.
    c. Adhere to recognized rules of documentation for sources.
(5) **Developing an awareness of relevance of the sociological skills to their lives and society.**
    a. Identify skills acquired as a sociology major.
    b. Recognize applicability of these skills to circumstances as a student, worker, family and community member, and citizen.
    c. Apply the sociological imagination to circumstances as a student, worker, family and community member, and citizen.

Figure 10.1 Assessment Goals (Sociology).

Developing Bibliographic and Information Literacy Objectives for the Sociology Major

After a review of the course syllabi, sociology textbooks, and reference sources, information literacy objectives were developed to support and coordinate with specific assessment goals (Figure 10.2).

While introductory courses may typically expect students to reach the application level of the Bloom's Taxonomy, the introductory course in the sociology discipline requires that some of the introductory-level learning objectives aim for the levels of analysis and synthesis. The capstone course requires that students reach the evaluation level of the taxonomy with the specific objectives requiring students to judge the value of a resource and to compare/contrast information from multiple sources. Some of the learning objectives suggest a graduated skill development, recognizing that students in an introductory course may reach the application level while students in a capstone course would be expected to operate at the evaluation level with the given objective. A sociology information literacy rubric (Figure 10.5) identifies the criteria to be met for proficiency at each cognitive level. The required cognitive level of skill development appears in the curriculum map that follows the objectives (Figure 10.3).

Developing the Bibliographic and Curriculum Outlines for the Introductory Seminar

The Assignment The assignment is tailor-made to assess information literacy acquisition. Students write a paper about the process of doing research for a self-selected sociology topic (e.g., divorce, youth crime) and are expected to reflect about their research as a sociologist would. They must compose four research questions and locate sources that provide information to answer those research questions. Their initial list of keywords intended to get them started in the research process is expected to grow as they continue with the project (keywords can be identified within the source material itself, or identified as indexing terms within a database or book index). It is also anticipated that students will identify additional sources of potential use with their review of the bibliographies for each source they encounter.

Bibliographic and Information Literacy Instruction There are two library instruction sessions. Near the beginning of the research process, the librarian introduces the students to both sociology sources and interdisciplinary sources appropriate for their sociology topics. For the majority of our instruction sessions, student topics or, at the least, topical areas, are identified prior to the session in order to direct the teaching to the students' specific research needs. Sources and the accompanying bibliographic skills include: the sociology subject guide on the library's Web page, scholarly sociology encyclopedias (with the recommendation to review the bibliography in the encyclopedia entry), books located in the library's online catalog, general/interdisciplinary and disciplinary indexes (including *Social Sciences Full Text*) (available in online subscription databases), sources for statistical information, and the identification of subject terms (controlled vocabulary).

I. **Related to Sociology Assessment Goals #2 & #5:**

Sociology Assessment Goal #2: Understanding how to collect and analyze sociological evidence/data, defined as the following:

a. Understand the range of sociological methods to gather data.

b. Understand which methods are appropriate to specific questions and areas of inquiry.

c. Understand how to read statistics, tables, graphs, to describe and summarize data, and to determine if it supports conclusions.

d. Understand how to use data in a logical argument to support conclusions.

Sociology Assessment Goal #5: Developing an awareness of relevance of the sociological skills to their lives and society.

a. Identify skills acquired as a sociology major.

b. Recognize applicability of these skills to circumstances as a student, worker, family and community member, and citizen.

c. Apply the sociological imagination to circumstances as a student, worker, family and community member, and citizen.

I. Objective A: Students will understand knowledge production for the sociology profession, including the ability to distinguish between primary and secondary literature.

I. Objective B: Students will identify and investigate standard sociology sources (both print and electronic) used for specific purposes. These will include reference sources for background reading (e.g., encyclopedias, guides, dictionaries, biographical sources, bibliographies, handbooks, yearbooks, almanacs, and atlases), book catalogs, statistical sources, legal sources, book review sources, subject indexes and abstracts of sociology journals, relevant disciplinary and interdisciplinary indexes and abstracts of scholarly and professional journals, relevant citation indexes, indexes to general periodicals, indexes to newspapers, and relevant sociology Web sites including the American Sociological Association's Web page.

I. Objective C: Students will use sources for relevant bibliographies, including specialized bibliographies in the relevant field, and bibliographies included in reference works, specialized books, essays, or journal articles.

I. Objective D: Students will recognize the difference between scholarly and professional journals and identify major sociology journals.

I. Objective E: Students will understand how government information is organized and identify the need to access information from municipal, state, federal, or international government sources, including utilizing the Congressional Research Service and U.S. Census Bureau publications.

I. Objective F: Students will recognize the interdisciplinary nature of sociology and identify the need for seeking information from other disciplines to support their research. In order to do this, students will distinguish between and appropriately use standard sociology sources and those sources outside of the profession.

I. Objective G: Students will determine whether to conduct an interview or survey and prepare by researching published sources.

I. Objective H: Students will compile a working bibliography by identifying a variety of types and formats of potential sources of information which may include published essays, books, articles, and interviews with experts in the field.

I. Objective I: Students will acquire needed material through means including interlibrary loan, and requesting material from a group such as a government agency, public interest group or organization.

II. **Related to Sociology Assessment Goal #3:**

Sociology Assessment Goal #3: Analyzing and applying sociological literature, defined as the following:

a. Understand social concepts and theories.

b. Summarize and explain literature in sociology.

c. Analyze and critique arguments in the sociology literature.

d. Apply relevant concepts to information and observations.

II. Objective A: Students will identify and document the potential usefulness of a source.

II. Objective B: Students will judge the value of a resource by noting its reliability, validity, accuracy, authority, timeliness, point of view or bias.

II. Objective C: Students will be able to compare/contrast information from multiple sources in order to ensure the accuracy of the information used.

III. **Related to Sociology Assessment Goal #4:**

Sociology Assessment Goal #4: Preparing presentations of data, argument and conclusions, defined as the following:

a. Communicate ideas effectively in oral and written forms.

b. Organize papers and presentations logically.

c. Adhere to recognized rules of documentation for sources.

III. Objective A: Students will describe the appropriate research process for the type of sociology paper to be written (i.e., social issue paper, critical evaluation of sociological literature, quantitative research paper, qualitative research paper).

III. Objective B: Students will understand economic, legal, and social issues surrounding the use of information and access and use information ethically and legally, including recognizing copyright laws. Students will appropriately acknowledge their sources according to the American Sociological Association's bibliographical format, including appropriately acknowledging quotations, accurately quoting, paraphrasing, and avoiding plagiarism.

Figure 10.2 Information Literacy Objectives (Sociology).

COURSE (bold designates core courses required for majors in Sociology)	LIBRARY IN-STRUCTION provided by Librarians for this course (∗)	INFORMATION LITERACY IDENTIFIED IN SYLLABI and/or in the COURSE DESCRIPTION (*Source for descriptions:* Rider University. *Undergraduate Catalog 06/07.* Lawrenceville, NJ: Rider University, 2006.)	SPECIFIC INFORMATION LITERACY SKILL(S) REQUIRED	COGNITIVE LEVEL OF INFORMATION LITERACY SKILL(S)
100-level-The Sociological Imagination (*Freshman level*)		*Course Description: In this introductory course, the student will learn the* "principles and concepts for the sociological analysis of human societies." *To be examined are the* "social relations, social structure, and institutions characteristic of societies past and present." *Considered are the causes and directions of social change.*	*NA=Not applicable; information literacy skills not relevant for this course*	
200-level-Introductory Seminar in Sociology (*Sophomore level*)	∗	*Course Description: This seminar* "locates sociology in relation to other disciplines; reviews the basic perspectives used by sociologists to study human behavior; and considers the methods and applications of sociological inquiry" *with an introduction to research and investigation skills.* Representative Assignment: Research project.	I. Objective A: [Cognitive levels: Comprehension and Application] I. Objective B: [Cognitive level: Application] I. Objective C: [Cognitive level: Application] I. Objective D: [Cognitive level: Comprehension] I. Objective E: [Cognitive level: Application] I. Objective F: [Cognitive level: Analysis and Synthesis] I. Objective G: [Cognitive level: Synthesis] I. Objective H: [Cognitive level: Application] II. Objective B: [Cognitive level: Application] III. Objective A: [Cognitive level: Application] III. Objective B: [Cognitive level: Application]	Comprehension Application Analysis Synthesis
300-level-Methods of Sociological Research (*Junior level*)		*Course Description:* "Builds upon the Introductory Seminar in Sociology. Social research methods using documents, observations, and questionnaires are taught, and used in completing research projects."	*Applying skills learned in the Introductory Seminar in Sociology (as appropriate).*	
300-level-Social Theory (*Junior level*)		*Course Description: Students will be introduced to the* "major thinkers and conceptual problems characterizing the development of sociological thought." Representative Assignment(s): Several written assignments requiring students to consult such sources as the Bureau of Labor Statistics, business journals, and legal cases (e.g., an alienation assignment requiring research about a particular occupation; students must identify sources of alienation within the job and apply Marxist theory to the alienation in the job).	*Applying skills learned in the Introductory Seminar in Sociology (as appropriate).*	

Figure 10.3 Curriculum Map (Sociology).

400-level- **Senior Seminar** **in Sociology** (*Senior level*)	*	*Course Description: In this seminar, students will be involved with the "in-depth examination and research of a specific issue of current importance in the discipline." The emphasis will be on "learning to do sociology."* Representative Assignment(s): Students are required to integrate the substantive knowledge and skills acquired in the sociology curriculum by completing a project in which the student demonstrates researching, writing and critical thinking skills.	I. Objective A: [Cognitive levels: Comprehension and Application] I. Objective B: [Cognitive level: Synthesis]. I. Objective C: [Cognitive level: Synthesis] I. Objective D: [Cognitive level: Application] I. Objective E: [Cognitive level: Synthesis] I. Objective F: [Cognitive level: Analysis and Synthesis] I. Objective G: [Cognitive level: Synthesis] I. Objective H: [Cognitive level: Application] I. Objective I: [Cognitive level: Synthesis] II. Objective A: [Cognitive level: Application and Analysis] II. Objective B: [Cognitive level: Evaluation] II. Objective C: [Cognitive level: Evaluation] III. Objective A: [Cognitive level: Application] III. Objective B: [Cognitive level: Application]	Comprehension Application Analysis Synthesis Evaluation
300-level *Electives:* 300-level-Cities and Suburbs (*Junior level*)	*	*Course Description: Students will examine the "growth of an urban way of life under the influence of industrialism" and make comparisons between urban and suburban areas. They will study the following institutions in cities: community, political, and economic.* Representative Assignment(s): Term project: Students will apply sociology research methods to an examination of urban and suburban areas.	*Applying skills learned in the Introductory Seminar in Sociology (as appropriate).*	
300-level-Social and Cultural Change (*Junior level*)		*Course Description: Students will investigate the "process of change in both industrial and nonindustrial settings. Particular attention is paid to the role of the individual in change as well as the roles played by the mode of production, social organization, and ideological constructs."* Representative Assignment(s): Term project/research assignment on a topic(s) of relevance to the course.	*Applying skills learned in the Introductory Seminar in Sociology (as appropriate).*	

Figure 10.3 (continued)

300-level-Law and the Legal Profession (*Junior level*)	*	*Course Description: Students will explore the "relationships between law, the economy, and the state." They will discuss "laws, legal systems and legal reasoning using cross-cultural comparisons and historical analysis of these in the United States." They will study "the impact of law on corporations, workers, women, and minorities."*	*Applying skills learned in the Introductory Seminar in Sociology (as appropriate).*
300-level-Social Inequality (*Junior level*)	*	*Course Description: Students will consider the "social, economic, and political aspects of the division of society into classes." They will examine "theories of stratification and the distribution of wealth, power, and prestige in societies past and present."* Representative Assignment(s): Term project (research includes using government publications).	*Applying skills learned in the Introductory Seminar in Sociology (as appropriate).*
300-level-Power and Politics (*Junior level*)		*Course Description: Students will examine the "nature and distribution of power in contemporary societies." They will analyze the "relationships between political processes and economic and social issues."* Representative Assignment(s): Research paper on a specific issue relevant to contemporary politics.	*Applying skills learned in the Introductory Seminar in Sociology (as appropriate).*

Figure 10.3 (continued)

A later instruction session introduces students to *Social Sciences Citation Index*, which is used by the students to identify the citations to one of the sources discovered during their research.

BIBLIOGRAPHIC OUTLINE

To support Objectives I. A, B, D, E, F, G, and H, students will be introduced to the following literature. In addition, Objectives II. B, and III. A and B are introduced in the introductory seminar. The following outline (as shown in Figure 10.4) partially follows the organization of "sources of information" in *The Sociology Student Writer's Manual* and includes representative titles. For descriptions of most of these titles and for additional bibliographic references, consult *The Sociology Student Writer's Manual* (Johnson, Rettig, Scott, and Garrison 2002, chapter 6) or *Sociology: A Guide to Reference and Information Sources* (Aby, Nalen, and Fielding, 2005).

Guides to Sociological Literature
  General Guides
  Specialized Guides
    Sociology: A Guide to Reference and Information Sources
  Handbooks
    Statistical Handbooks
      Statistical Abstract of the United States
      County and City Data Book
      Historical Statistics of the United States: Colonial Times to 1970
    Subject Handbooks
  Yearbooks
    Statistical Yearbooks
      Demographic Yearbook
      Sourcebook on Criminal Justice Statistics
      Statistical Yearbook
      Vital Statistics of the United States
      Uniform Crime Reports for the United States
    Subject Yearbooks
      Annual Review of Sociology
  Subject Dictionaries and Encyclopedias
    Subject Dictionaries
      The Blackwell Dictionary of Sociology: A User's Guide to Sociological Language
    Encyclopedias
      The Continuum Complete International Encyclopedia of Sexuality
      Encyclopedia of American Crime and Justice
      Encyclopedia of Child Abuse
      Encyclopedia of Social Theory
      Encyclopedia of Sociology
  Indexes and Abstracts
    Online Database Systems
      ABI/INFORM
      ERIC
      PsycINFO
    Disciplinary Indexes
      Social Sciences Full Text
    Topical Indexes
      Population Index
      The Gallup Poll Cumulative Index: Public Opinion, 1935–1997
    Citation Indexes
      Social Sciences Citation Index
    Disciplinary Abstracts
      Sociological Abstracts (Socio File)
    Specialized Abstracts
      Criminal Justice Abstracts
      Women's Studies Abstracts
  Bibliographies
    Appended Bibliographies (i.e., citations in an article or book)
    Book-length Bibliographies

Periodicals and Newspapers
  General Periodicals
  Newspapers
  Academic Journals
    Scholarly Journals
      American Journal of Sociology
      American Sociological Review
    Professional Journals (see the *Sociology Student Writer's Manual* for an extensive title listing)
      Aging and Society
      American Demographics
      Public Health Reports
      Women and Work

Figure 10.4 Bibliographic Outline (Sociology).

Researching Books
    Book Review Sources
    Catalogs of Libraries
U.S. Government Publications
    General Publications
        Catalog of United States Government Publications (http://catalog.gpo.gov)
    U.S. Census Bureau Publications
Sociology Associations
    American Sociological Association (http://www.asanet.org)
World Wide Web Sources for Sociology Research
    Public Opinion sources
        Gallup Poll (http://www.galluppoll.com)
        PollingReport.com (Trends in American Public Opinion) (http://www.pollingreport.com)
    Statistics
        Statistical Resources on the Web/Sociology
        (University of Michigan) (http://www.lib.umich.edu/govdocs/stsoc.html)

Figure 10.4 (continued)

ASSESSING THE INFORMATION LITERACY SKILLS

Formal assessment is scheduled to occur at two levels, at the conclusion of the 200-level introductory seminar and at the conclusion of the 400-level senior seminar. At the intermediate, 300-level, course-embedded information literacy skills will be taught as appropriate to reinforce the skills learned in the introductory seminar. Student research plans and librarian responses will be prepared as appropriate. Sociology professors will determine the effectiveness of the students' research process based upon the resulting products (e.g., papers, term projects). Recommendations from the sociology professors for reinforcement of specific information literacy skills will be provided at each level to the librarians who will be reinforcing the skills in the 400-level Senior Seminar in Sociology.

"Getting it right" at the introductory level is essential for the future success of students in the senior seminar. A pilot of the assessment of information literacy skills for the introductory seminar follows, revealing several areas that required strengthening in the teaching and learning process.

Pilot of the Assessment Process

At the conclusion of the introductory seminar, ten student papers were selected randomly and were provided to the librarian providing the instruction. The Sociology Bibliographic & Information Literacy Rubric (Figure 10.5) was used to determine the proficiency levels reached. Of consideration in the process were several observations. For example, was the student's use of the "free Web" appropriate to the sociology assignment? Do the students recognize the difference between these "free Web" sources and the subscription databases? How many students used *Statistical Abstracts* or a similar statistical source (*Objective I. B*)? Did the student appropriately utilize the most effective subscription databases for access to journal articles (*Objective I. F*)?

In the process of reviewing the working bibliography, we noted whether the students had identified keywords in the indexes or tables of contents of books, within the text of articles, or within the controlled vocabulary of the databases. Was the research process

SOC-200-Introductory Seminar in Sociology

A sample size of 10 student papers was reviewed to determine the proficiency level of the bibliographic and information literacy objectives below.

INFORMATION LITERACY OBJECTIVES	COGNITIVE LEVEL EXPECTED by Course level	WEAK 0–1	ALMOST 2	PROFICIENT 3 (criteria are for SOC-200)	EXCEPTIONAL 4
I. Objective A: Students will understand knowledge production for the sociology profession, including the ability to distinguish between primary and secondary types of research.	SOC-200—*Comprehension & Application* 300-Level courses (*skill reinforced as appropriate*) SOC-400—*Comprehension & Application*			I.A. Minimum expectation to be considered <u>Proficient</u> at the <u>Application</u> level: Students will correctly note the source type (i.e., primary, secondary) in the research paper.	
I. Objective B: Students will identify and investigate standard sociology sources (both print and electronic) used for specific purposes. These will include reference sources for background reading (e.g., encyclopedias, guides, dictionaries, biographical sources, bibliographies, handbooks, yearbooks, almanacs, and atlases), book catalogs, statistical sources, legal sources, book review sources, subject indexes and abstracts of sociology journals, relevant disciplinary and interdisciplinary indexes and abstracts of scholarly and professional journals, relevant citation indexes, indexes to general periodicals, indexes to newspapers, and relevant sociology Web sites including the American Sociological Association's Web page.	SOC-200—*Application* 300-Level courses (*skill reinforced as appropriate*) SOC-400—*Synthesis*			I.B. Minimum expectation to be considered <u>Proficient</u> at the <u>Application</u> level: A broad use of Sociology sources appropriate for the topic of the research paper will be identified.	
I. Objective C: Students will use sources for relevant bibliographies, including specialized bibliographies in the relevant field, and bibliographies included in reference works, specialized books, essays, or journal articles.	SOC-200—*Application* 300-Level courses (*skill reinforced as appropriate*) SOC-400—*Synthesis*			I.C. Minimum expectation to be considered <u>Proficient</u> at the <u>Application</u> level: Students will note whether they have used bibliographies in monographic format, discovered in books, discovered in journal articles.	
I. Objective D: Students will recognize the difference between scholarly and professional journals and identify major sociology journals.	SOC-200—*Comprehension* 300-Level courses (*skill reinforced as appropriate*) SOC-400—*Application*			I.D. Minimum expectation to be considered <u>Proficient</u> at the <u>Comprehension</u> level: Students will note whether the source is intended for a general audience, professional audience, scholarly audience, and will specifically identify sociology journals.	

Figure 10.5 Sociology Bibliographic & Information Literacy Rubric.

I. Objective E: Students will understand how government information is organized and identify the need to access information from municipal, state, federal, or international government sources, including utilizing the Congressional Research Service and U.S. Census Bureau publications.	SOC-200— *Application* 300-Level courses (*skill reinforced as appropriate*) SOC-400— *Synthesis*	I.E. Minimum expectation to be considered <u>Proficient</u> at the <u>Application</u> level: Where appropriate, government sources will be utilized and identified as such.
I. Objective F: Students will recognize the interdisciplinary nature of sociology and identify the need for seeking information from other disciplines to support their research. In order to do this, students will distinguish between and appropriately use standard sociology sources and those sources outside of the profession.	SOC-200— *Analysis & Synthesis* 300-Level courses (*skill reinforced as appropriate*) SOC-400— *Analysis & Synthesis*	I.F. Minimum expectation to be considered <u>Proficient</u> at the <u>Synthesis</u> level: Students will distinguish between sociology sources and those written for a specific discipline, will recognize the need to pursue sources in a specific discipline, and will research and utilize sources in the identified discipline.
I. Objective G: Students will determine whether to conduct an interview or survey and prepare by researching published sources.	SOC-200— *Synthesis* 300-Level courses (*skill reinforced as appropriate*) SOC-400— *Synthesis*	I.G. Minimum expectation to be considered <u>Proficient</u> at the <u>Synthesis</u> level: Where necessary, students will conduct an interview and appropriately perform the preparatory research.
I. Objective H: Students will compile a working bibliography by identifying a variety of types and formats of potential sources of information which may include published essays, books, articles, and interviews with experts in the field.	SOC-200— *Application* 300-Level courses (*skill reinforced as appropriate*) SOC-400— *Application*	I.H. Minimum expectation to be considered <u>Proficient</u> at the <u>Application</u> level: The student's bibliography will identify a variety of types and formats of sources.
I. Objective I: Students will acquire needed material through means including interlibrary loan, and requesting material from a group such as a government agency, public interest group or organization.	SOC-400— *Synthesis*	
II. Objective A: Students will identify and document the potential usefulness of a source.	SOC-400— *Application & Analysis*	
II. Objective B: Students will judge the value of a resource by noting its reliability, validity, accuracy, authority, timeliness, point of view or bias.	SOC-200— *Application* 300-Level courses (*skill reinforced as appropriate*) SOC-400— *Evaluation*	II.B. Minimum expectation to be considered <u>Proficient</u> at the <u>Application</u> level: Students will note reliability, validity, accuracy, authority, timeliness, point of view or bias.

Figure 10.5 (continued)

II. Objective C: Students will be able to compare/contrast information from multiple sources in order to ensure the accuracy of the information used.	SOC-400— *Analysis, Synthesis, & Evaluation*	
III. Objective A: Students will describe the appropriate research process for the type of sociology paper to be written (i.e., social issue paper, critical evaluation of sociological literature, quantitative research paper, qualitative research paper).	SOC-200— *Application* 300-Level courses (*skill reinforced as appropriate*) SOC-400— *Application*	III.A. Minimum expectation to be considered <u>Proficient</u> at the <u>Application</u> level: The type of sociology paper will be identified and the appropriate research process will be conducted.
III. Objective B: Students will understand economic, legal, and social issues surrounding the use of information and access and use information ethically and legally, including recognizing copyright laws. Students will appropriately acknowledge their sources according to the American Sociological Association's bibliographical format, including appropriately acknowledging quotations, accurately quoting, paraphrasing, and avoiding plagiarism.	SOC-200— *Application* 300-Level courses (*skill reinforced as appropriate*) SOC-400— *Application*	III.B. Minimum expectation to be considered <u>Proficient</u> at the <u>Application</u> level: Sources will be properly acknowledged according to bibliographic style requirements.

Figure 10.5 (continued)

a "one-stop shopping" (one trip only to the library) or circular (returning to the library multiple times for resources)? While narrowing the search, did the source information contribute positively to the narrowing of the search or did the student continue to have difficulty narrowing the search (and the amount of material gathered hindered the narrowing process)? Did the student identify transferable skills from a library instruction session for a different course (e.g., Research Writing, a law class)? Did the student recognize the benefit of asking a librarian for help (while not a necessary step, we noted when students had benefited from this and when they could have benefited from a consultation with a librarian)? Did the student learn to ask good questions? Was there recognition of the organization of the library's collections (e.g., subject arrangement of books)? Were any frustrations with the research process noted? Was creativity exhibited in the search process (i.e., one student watched a topic-related TV program and the TV station Web site led her to a related book)? Did the student understand the connection of *Social Sciences Citation Index* (*SSCI*) to the research assignment (*Objective I. H*)?

Did the student note the date of the material and recognize the need for more current information (e.g., one student noted locating information from the 1950s for divorce research; another noted statistics on crime gathered from the 1980s and 1990s)? Did the student note the importance of the author's credentials (e.g., some realized this during the *SSCI* search)? Did the student question the credibility of a source (e.g., one student noted concern about the credibility of the sources borrowed from a roommate's personal collection) (*Objective II. B and C*)? How solid is the Works Cited page (*Objective III. B*)?

Reviewing the Assessment Results

Student Learning of Information Literacy Skills. Of particular interest was the recognition by the students that research is a *process*. Only one student approached this with a "one-stop" approach (gathering all of the resources in one library visit), while most made repeated visits to the library as they identified the need for additional sources to answer their research questions. Many utilized the book collection as an initial approach and emphasized browsing and recognition of Library of Congress subject areas. Some noted having asked librarians for assistance. Most were keenly aware of the purpose of the librarian-assisted search session with *Social Sciences Citation Index* and recognized the significance of the author's work having been cited.

Some noted for themselves a connection between the skills learned in the Research Writing class or in a library instruction session for a law class. One student had learned to check the author's credentials in the Research Writing section that she was in and transferred this skill to the research process for her sociology course. Others successfully questioned the credibility of the information based on the author's credentials or the relevance of the information based on its date.

Based on the proficiency levels identified within each paper for each information literacy objective, data was gathered to enable a programmatic, or aggregated, view of the proficiency level(s), as described in the Introduction. In the summary of the data describing the students' proficiency levels (Figure 10.6), the rows are organized by the

Information Literacy Objectives	Student Paper #1	Student Paper #2	Student Paper #3	Student Paper #4	Student Paper #5	Student Paper #6	Student Paper #7	Student Paper #8	Student Paper #9	Student Paper #10	Mean Score
I. A.	NA	NA	NA	NA	NA	NA	NA	NA	NA	NA	NA
I. B.	2	2	1	1	0	1	2	2	2	2	1.5
I. C.	1	1	0	3	0	1	0	1.5	3	0	1.05
I. D.	1	2	0	1.5	0	1	2	1.5	2	0	1.1
I. E.	NA	1.5	NA	NA	NA	NA	NA	NA	NA	2	-
I. F.	1	1	0	1	1	1	2.5	2	1.5	1	1.2
I. G.	NA	NA	NA	NA	NA	NA	NA	NA	NA	NA	NA
I. H.	3	1.5	1	3	1	1	2.5	3	3	3	2.2
I. I.	NA	NA	NA	NA	NA	NA	NA	NA	NA	NA	NA
II. A.	NA	NA	NA	NA	NA	NA	NA	NA	NA	NA	NA
II. B.	0	2	1	0	3	3	2	1	3	3	1.8
II. C.	NA	NA	NA	NA	NA	NA	NA	NA	NA	NA	NA
III. A.	NA	NA	NA	NA	NA	NA	NA	NA	NA	NA	NA
III. B.	2.5	2	2.75	3	MISSING	3	1	3	3	3	2.58

NA = Not applicable as this objective was either not taught or not required during the library instruction session or is an objective intended for the senior seminar.

Figure 10.6 SOC-200–Information Literacy Objectives: Proficiency Rankings.

sociology information literacy objectives. In reviewing each student paper (the columns), if the student has met the criteria for "proficient," a "3" is assigned to the objective for that student's paper. Otherwise, the appropriate number is assigned to the objective. Once all of the papers have been assigned a proficiency level for each objective, a mean score is determined for each objective from all of the papers. This mean score becomes the identification of the proficiency level in the aggregate for each information literacy objective. By reviewing the aggregated proficiency levels, librarians can, thus, identify information literacy objectives that require more attention in their teaching.

Comments on the Results

Some of the objectives were not taught in the library instruction session, but will be in the future (i.e., *Objective I. A*). Of biggest concern was the students' database selection. There was a dependence upon general audience/interdisciplinary databases (e.g., *Academic Search Premier* or *Wilson Omnifile*) and an interdisciplinary archive (*JSTOR*). There seemed to be a lack of awareness of databases that may have been more appropriate (e.g., while recognizing that journals fell into the categories of psychology or marketing, it would be a logical decision to redirect the search in one of those directions by pursuing information in *PsycINFO*, *PsycARTICLES* or *ABI-Inform*. If the decision was made to use gender as a focus, it would be logical to use a database such as *GenderWatch*). Students are introduced to the differences between a general audience database and a subject-specific database in the freshman Research Writing course and this is the stage to reinforce their use of subject-specific indexed databases.

Recommendations to Improve the Teaching and Learning Process

The proposals are intended as guidance and it is expected that librarians will adapt the recommendations to create an approach that is most appropriate for the working relationship between the librarians and the professors. The objectives were agreed to by the sociology professors and the library liaison to the Sociology Department. The liaison became more involved by attending classes early in the semester to enhance his understanding of the course, and by incorporating additional working research sessions for the students during the semester. However, he decided against utilizing the research plan and, instead, to provide verbal feedback to the students over the course of the semester. Some of the data indicated that student papers would have benefited from the use of additional sources. In the future, the process will be formalized with written feedback from the librarian to the student. This will also provide a record for both the student and the sociology professor of the librarian–student interaction and that record can be incorporated into the determination of the final grade.

From the data, we can recommend that the learning objectives that require emphasis in order to improve student learning are Objectives: I. B, I. C, I. D, I. E., I. F., II. B. Reinforcement is needed for subject-specific indexed databases, including *Social Sciences Full Text* (which none of the sample papers referenced). Students need to recognize whether the source is intended for a general audience, professional audience, or scholarly audience, and be able to identify sociology journals (Objectives I. B, I. D, & I. F). More emphasis needs to be given to the organization of government information and the usefulness of government sources for data (I. E), statistical sources such as *Statistical Abstracts* (I. B, I. E), the use of bibliographies (I. C), and the evaluation of information (e.g., noting timeliness, authors' credentials, etc.) (II. B). Reinforcement is also needed of skills learned in Research Writing.

CONCLUSION

Our approach to assessment focuses on improving the teaching and learning process. The first step requires understanding what the students are learning in order to make teaching changes that improve learning outcomes. This process requires an understanding of the discipline in order to develop disciplinary information literacy objectives and also requires close collaboration with disciplinary faculty since the teaching of information literacy must be shared between librarians and disciplinary faculty.

The next step for sociology will be to identify the learning outcomes for students in the senior seminar, make teaching improvements in the information literacy curriculum for both the introductory and senior seminars, and, then, to expect improvements in student learning.

From our initial experience of assessing Research Writing (Warner, in press), we know to expect these improvements. Our respect for the built-in assessment process has vastly improved a library instruction program that was already considered successful. But now our approach is wiser and more targeted, and those who benefit the most are our students.

REFERENCES

Rider University. *Undergraduate Catalog 06/07*. Lawrenceville, NJ: Rider University, 2006.

Truchil, Barry. *Assessment Report of the Sociology Department*. Lawrenceville, NJ: Rider University, 2006.

Warner, Dorothy. "Programmatic Assessment of Information Literacy Skills Using Rubrics." *Journal on Excellence in College Teaching* (in press).

ADDITIONAL SOURCES

Aby, Stephen H. James Nalen, and Lori Fielding. *Sociology: A Guide to Reference and Information Sources* (3rd ed.). Westport, CT: Libraries Unlimited, 2005.

Johnson, William A., Jr., Richard P. Rettig, Gregory M. Scott, and Stephen M. Garrison. *The Sociology Student Writer's Manual* (3rd ed.). Upper Saddle River, NJ: Prentice Hall, 2002.

Proctor, Lesley, Richard Wartho, and Meghan Anderson. "Embedding Information Literacy in the Sociology Program at the University of Otago." *Australian Academic & Research Libraries* 36(4) (December 2005): 153–168.

Index

About the Author

DOROTHY ANNE WARNER is Professor-Librarian and Library Instruction Co-Coordinator at Rider University.

DATE DUE

DEMCO, INC. 38-2931